START AN COSMETIC INJECTABLE PRACTICE

START AND GROW YOUR COSMETIC INJECTABLE PRACTICE

PRACTICAL AND AFFORDABLE STRATEGIES NEEDED TO ADD FACIAL INJECTABLES TO YOUR PRACTICE

Gigi Meinecke

Copyright © 2020 FACES, LLC
All rights reserved.

No part of this publication may be reproduced, distributed, or transmitted in any form or by any means, including, but not limited to photocopying, recording, or other electronic or mechanical methods, without the prior written permission of the author.
For permission requests write to the author at:
Attention Permissions Coordinator
info@estheticseminars.com

Important Disclaimer:

This publication contains materials designed to assist readers in establishing a facial injectable practice and is for educational purposes only. While the author has made every attempt to verify that the information provided in this book is correct and up to date, the reader/user assumes full and sole responsibility for the use and application of the techniques and/or procedures. The author is not offering it as legal, accounting, or other professional services advice. Best efforts have been used in preparing this book, however, the author makes no representations or warranties of any kind and assumes no liability of any kind with respect to the accuracy or completeness of the contents and specifically disclaims any implied warranties of merchantability or fitness of use for a particular purpose. The advice, examples, and strategies contained herein are not suitable for every situation. The materials contained herein are not intended to represent or guarantee that the reader/user will achieve the desired results and the author makes no such guarantee. The author shall not be held liable or responsible to any person or entity with respect to any loss or incidental or consequential damages caused, or alleged to have been caused, directly or indirectly, by the reader/user's reliance upon or application of information programs contained herein. Success is determined by factors beyond the control of the author including but not limited to, market conditions, reader/user effort levels and educational background. No warranty may be created or extended by sales representatives or written sales materials. Every company is different and the advice and strategies contained herein may not be suitable for your situation. This book is not intended for use as a source of legal or financial advice. Evaluating and launching a business involves complex legal and financial issues. All practitioners should retain competent legal and financial professionals to provide guidance in evaluating and pursuing a specific business idea

.

Printed in the United States of America
First Edition

DEDICATION:

This book is dedicated to my husband and son
— the two people who are my world.

Table of Contents

Chapter 1 1
IS THIS BOOK FOR YOU? 1
   Chapter 2 3
ROI OF TRAINING 3
   Chapter 3 9
STAFF EDUCATION 9
   Chapter 4 13
PRACTICE DECOR 13
   Chapter 5 20
YOUR COSMETIC PRACTICE WARDROBE 20
   Chapter 6 24
OVERHEAD CONTROL 24
   Chapter 7 32
GRAY MARKET PRODUCTS 32
   Chapter 8 34
CREATING YOUR FEE SCHEDULE 34
   Chapter 9 38
SCHEDULING INJECTABLE PATIENTS 38
   Chapter 10 44
DISCOUNTS 44

Chapter 11 46
TREATING YOUR STAFF 46
Chapter 12 50
CONSULTATION AND PATIENT SELECTION 50
Chapter 13 56
KNOW YOUR LIMITATIONS 56
Chapter 14 59
PHOTODOCUMENTATION 59
Chapter 15 63
THE DISSATISFIED PATIENT 63
Chapter 16 67
JOIN THE GROUP 67
Chapter 17 70
CREATING PATIENT AWARENESS 70
Chapter 18 72
MARKETING TO YOUR EXISTING BASE 72
Chapter 19 75
EMAIL MARKETING 75
Chapter 20 79
YOUR WEBSITE 79
Chapter 21 82
ONLINE REVIEWS 82
Chapter 22 87
SOCIAL MEDIA 87

Chapter 23 94
SOCIAL MEDIA CONTENT CREATION 94
    Chapter 24 98
STAFF AND SOCIAL NETWORKING 98
    Chapter 25 101
SOCIAL MEDIA PLATFORM RULES 101
    Chapter 26 104
PATIENT PRIVACY 104
    Chapter 27 107
5 IMMUTABLE RULES 107
    Chapter 28 112
LET'S GO! 112

Chapter 1

IS THIS BOOK FOR YOU?

Whether you're a licensed healthcare provider thinking about adding facial injectables to your existing practice or you've already completed training and want to know how to get things started, this book is for you.

Who am I? I'm a non-core specialist with degrees in dentistry and nursing. My practice is located in a highly competitive market with a rich density of cosmetic core-specialists (plastic and dermatology) - as well as dentists. I've never paid for advertising, never used social coupons and never invested a dime in Search Engine Optimization (SEO). Yet, half of my practice is dedicated to injectable treatments. How did this happen and what's the secret to producing this type of growth?

In the following pages I'll walk you through what it takes to build a successful injectable practice without losing your shirt. From basic equipment to patient management to social media advertising - you'll find out how to structure and manage these and other fundamental parameters to fuel practice growth.

When I started offering cosmetic treatments, my existing dental practice was mature and doing well. Adding injectables was not a "rescue operation." My facial injectable practice was borne out of interest expressed by a few of my dental patients (although, to be fair, demonstrable enthusiasm was not fully established) and sheer subject matter passion on my end. I had no budget (nor appetite) for paid marketing. And, given the small number of patients I *thought* I'd be treating, in order to make this work I couldn't overspend, overstock, overstaff, overestimate or overreach. This forced me to be careful with every expenditure. I never set out to create a cosmetic practice that would equal or eclipse my dental practice. But by applying the principles outlined in this book, I see now, it was inevitable.

"Waste neither time nor money, but make the best use of both" Ben Franklin

Chapter 2

ROI OF TRAINING

"Continuous learning is the minimum requirement for success in any field." Brian Tracy

You can do everything else right, but if your training is sub-par your skills will be sub-par. You can only be as good as your training and experience. Facial injectables is a completely novel area for most general practitioners and non-core specialists. For many of us the pertinent anatomy was learned and, in some cases, forgotten years ago. Some practitioners haven't given an injection since their days of training. In addition to facial aging and understanding beauty, the skill of injections has to be (re-)learned. Finding quality training can be a hit or miss proposition. How do you figure out which program is best? Word of mouth might be helpful, but more often than not, people have no basis for comparison. Evaluating something requires a standard by which to measure its quality. Anything can seem great when it's your only exposure.

When planning any new purchase, it's reasonable to do some research beforehand. First, find out exactly what's covered in the conference you're considering. With respect to subject matter, educational providers vary widely in the number of areas they cover in beginner courses. Don't be fooled by price because it's not an indicator. In fact, some of the more expensive programs cover significantly fewer areas than those that are nearly half the price. Before committing any resources to enrollment, make sure you do a comparison to see exactly what's included in the curriculum.

Next, determine if the program is live or online. Understand that online courses are not well suited to content that requires hands-on learning.[1] Since facial injectables is a relatively young field, the science behind it and treatment delivery techniques evolve and change monthly. The biggest problem with online training is information obsolescence. No sooner has a program gone through editing and video production that its content is already outdated. The skeptic in you might be thinking: "seriously? how much can lip injection techniques change over time?" Trust me, it can and does. And bear in mind that the protocol for vascular occlusion (a potential dermal filler adverse event) has changed dramatically over the last 2 years and is likely to continue to evolve at this rapid pace as the field progresses.

In addition to presenting antiquated information, the videos are often lengthy - as in hours and hours. I've had doctors tell me that after paying full freight for an online training module they ultimately gave up because it was taking too long to complete. Marketers of online programs want you to believe that "On Demand" courses save you time away from the office. But the sad reality is that education and technology researchers have shown the average completion rate for massive open online courses (MOOCs) to be as low as 15%.[2]

---

[1] https://www.theptdc.com/online-classes-or-in-person-workshops-for-ceus
[2] https://www.influencive.com/why-no-one-finishes-online-courses

Online content has no deadlines and people wind up procrastinating. Don't make the costly mistake of wasting time and money on an obsolete program that you'll probably never complete.

How much anatomy is included? Safe and successful facial injectable treatment is entirely predicated on understanding detailed anatomy. Further, it's not enough to know that a structure is located in the cheek. You need to know its depth, what's above it and below it. To that end, safe injectors require a full appreciation of the 3-dimensional facial envelope. Books are helpful but they only offer 2 dimensions. Cadaver anatomy is the gold standard when it comes to a complete understanding the face and its structural arrangement.

Is the program rooted in the scientific literature? This one is tricky. As previously stated, any training seems adequate when you've had no prior exposure to a subject. Without instruction from two completely different organizations it's impossible to say whether something is good, adequate or lousy. It's frightening to see how many groups advertise procedures and techniques that are not only unsupported by the literature but in some cases unequivocally contraindicated. Unfortunately, endorsement of CME, PACE or CERP doesn't guarantee accuracy of content so it's of little value here. One thing is certain, if a didactic course is only offered via on-demand format it's very unlikely that the program closely adheres to scientific literature. Remember, this is an evolving field with protocols and techniques changing monthly. Consider video formatting a red flag since costs associated with regular editing and updating are prohibitive.

UPSELL-UCATION

Beware of programs that exist solely to *sell* CME rather than educate. Some teaching groups might appear legitimate, but their goal is to provide minimal information leading you along a path of continuous financial outlay. They function like a slot machine in Vegas, giving you just enough payout to keep you coming back. Your desire to learn and incorporate injectables without knowledge gaps, coupled with their slick marketing tactics keeps you on the hook and enrolling in their next level course - and the next and the next. Don't fall prey to the up-sell psychology. Do your homework. There are plenty of courses that provide extensive coverage of multiple areas in single programs - often for less money. When CME advertisements look more like infomercials selling ShamWow or Ginsu Knives, just move along...nothing to see here. Likewise, think twice before enrolling when you see CME/CE ads containing classic "upsell" words such as: *Amazing, Biggest, Bonus, Imagine, Incredible, Now, or Save!* These are marketing terms used by common merchandising businesses - unrelated to healthcare. Serious education providers rarely resort to these coarse marketing ploys.

The best education will teach you how to think, not just how to do.

Quality education, naturally, relies heavily on the student himself. Without a willing participant no amount of educational excellence will do any good. Aside from an engaged pupil, other requisite elements of exceptional education are the quality of the teaching staff and the program content.[3] Large teaching organizations, by design, have to employ faculty in numbers sufficient to support their audiences.

[3] Husain Salilul Akareem & Syed Shahadat Hossain (2016) Determinants of education quality: what makes students' perception different?, **Open Review of Educational Research**, 3:1, 52-67, DOI: 10.1080/23265507.2016.1155167

Unless these instructors have academic associations with medical, dental or nursing schools, they're usually individuals aspiring to become speakers with no other special qualifications. Therefore, the quality of these trainers is generally a hit-or-miss proposition with no true way to measure their skills as educators or subject matter experts. If you decide to try one of the large organizations, you're within your right to find out who the instructor will be before registering. Once you know their name, Google them and do your own inquiry. If they haven't published anything, have no academic institution affiliations and appear only to be in private practice you should reconsider your enrollment.

Although he was talking about something slightly different, the phrase "Content is King" by Bill Gates is applicable to many areas. As mentioned, many businesses - including some that teach - use a "Funnel" approach to keep you on the sales hook. The Marketing Funnel is a consumer buying scheme that works by moving you along from one purchase to the next. Unfortunately, it's how some teaching organizations operate. Each seminar doles out just enough content to entice you into signing up (and paying) for the next one. The lesson here is to identify injectable instruction programs that deliver the highest quality content for the most reasonable price.

TRAINING PROGRAM CRITERIA SUMMARY:

- Compare the number of facial areas covered with similar courses
- Avoid on-demand (pre-recorded) programs
- Look for programs predicated on anatomy (preferably cadaver review workshops)

- Before enrollment, ask for the name of the instructor who will teach at **that event** - research that person
- Beware of programs using low-end retail wording (*Bonus, Incredible, Save, Amazing, etc.*)
- Compare enrollment fees - more expensive doesn't always mean more content

Chapter 3

STAFF EDUCATION

"One man can be a crucial ingredient on a team, but one man cannot make a team." Kareem Abdul-Jabbar

Especially in the early stages of injectable practice development, one of the most important ingredients of success is having your staff understand the nuts, bolts and nuances associated with the procedures you'll be doing. Think about the treatments you already offer in your practice. Your staff has seen these procedures and all the associated follow up appointments, thousands of times. That methodical repetition is what allows staff to become fluent when talking about those treatments. Fluency comes into play during those times when you're not in the treatment room and the staff is alone with the patient. As a rule, that's the time when patients wind up asking all manner of questions about the procedure they're about to have. With services you provide regularly, your staff can answer these questions fully and with authority, based on their experience working at your side. This ability to respond to questions fully and knowledgeably provides the patient with powerful subliminal clues about you and your expertise. It inspires patient confidence because it confirms that you perform that procedure regularly.

Don't underestimate the power of obvious teamwork. It doesn't go unnoticed when a practitioner and assistant work together like a well-oiled machine. Humans are highly attuned to non-verbal cues and can detect even the most subtle shift in composure. All procedures you do should be well-choreographed. Fluid movements all but confirm mastery and frictionless synergy can be almost hypnotic for patients. This extends to having all necessary supplies within reach during treatment. When staff has to dash out of the treatment room in the middle of a procedure to fetch a needed item, it suggests at best, lack of preparedness and at worst, incompetence. Without proper instruction, it's not the staff's fault if your treatment room isn't set up properly. Especially in the early stages, whenever possible, you should keep all supplies related to injectables in the room(s) where you'll be treating those patients.

Live patient treatment exercises at training sessions allow staff to see and experience the procedural mechanics and develop an understanding of their role. They may even have the opportunity to rehearse their "part" at the event before "going live" in your office. Support personnel registration fees are usually very reasonable in the field of injectables. Don't be a cheapskate. Before you dismiss the idea of including them, think of what it will save you in time and aggravation. If staff doesn't attend the program, *you* become the instructor when you return to the office. Be honest with yourself and decide if your time is well spent teaching staff. Moreover, at this early stage of your injectable education, does your depth of knowledge in the field make *you* the best teacher?

Sometimes, circumstances don't allow for staff course attendance. In absence of formal training the next best approach to getting everyone on board is to do an office "technical rehearsal." This is something that stage actors do to make sure everything works and there's enough room on the set to execute the scene. For example, some procedures, such as Kybella treatment, are time sensitive. Actual injection time for Kybella should be 2 minutes or less due to the fact that the patient will experience a burning sensation beginning at the 2-minute mark. When I decided to add Kybella to my office injectable menu I did a technical rehearsal with my staff the day before our first patient. It may seem goofy while you're going through the motions but it's remarkably useful in identifying the small things that can make a procedure appear seamless. It also reinforces any "absolute necessities" associated with specific procedures, such as timing. Patients know when a practitioner and assistant work synergistically - the practitioner barely needs to speak and the movements between them are effortless and smooth.

OFFICE EFFICIENCIES AND ENERGY

Knowing what supplies to order and in what quantity may sound like low level details but data suggests that it may represent a significant early obstacle for those wanting to launch an injectable practice. Most injectable teaching organizations offer a handout containing a list of preferred vendors, so you at least have a starting point. But unless your staff is present during training don't expect them to be able to intuit what's needed and in what quantity to get an injectable practice up and running. Here's a link to receive a list of what you need for each treatment modality: **bit.ly/PracticeForms** This entry level supply list will get you started without breaking the bank. Print it out and hand it to the person in charge of supplies as soon as you return from training.

In addition to knowing how a procedure is performed and what to expect as it's carried out, well-structured training helps front desk personnel field phone inquiries as well. It's especially helpful for calls your office may receive within hours or days after a treatment. Educating staff on what kind of information a practitioner needs to make decisions and/or recommendations for common injectable problems saves time on your end and frustration on the patients end. Instead of a volley of phone calls back and forth, well trained staff can cut to the chase and efficiently get all the necessary details at the first point of contact. The bottom line is that untrained employees create inefficiencies that are a financial burden to the practice. In the world of injectables and medicine as a whole, the cost-benefit ratio for staff training is overwhelmingly positive.

Another intangible benefit to including staff in training courses you attend, is that the excitement of new procedures (particularly ones that might benefit your staff personally - more on that later) creates a buzz in the entire office. Anyone who's been in practice for even a few years knows that a new skill is often a breath of fresh air and can reinvigorate your sense of purpose and professional fulfillment. Staff feels this too. Employees included in training feel valued. In addition to increasing their job-satisfaction, they become engaged. The difference between satisfaction and engagement is ultimately a commitment to the practice mission. Statistics published by Dale Carnegie Training (2016) also show that companies with engaged employees outperform those without by 202%.

In addition to improving business efficiencies, Including staff in training boosts office morale. This translates to a more polished patient experience. Happy patients become ambassadors for you and your practice.

Chapter 4

PRACTICE DECOR

"The best rooms also have something to say about the people who live in them." David Hicks

As a practitioner, you are your Brand. Therefore, everything about you: your personality, your voice, your attitude, your clothing, your office and its ambiance, its furnishings, - they're all part of that Brand.

On a day when you're not working, walk into your practice and have a look around. Try to experience the space as if you were a new patient. Sit in patient designated areas and view the office from angles you normally don't see. What sort of impression do you think your patient's get from the surroundings? Be honest, do you believe it looks like an office that delivers high-end, fee-for-service cosmetic treatments? If the overall impression is that of a dark living room from the 1970's or cluttered and folksy like the inside of a craft store it's doubtful you'll be able to attract the type of clientele who are interested in cosmetic treatments. Facial injectables are not a necessity, which is often in contrast to your existing menu of treatment items as a non-core specialist. Cosmetic treatment is by definition, a luxury item.

Let's take this a bit further. When I say the word "beach" what sort of imagery comes to mind? For most people it triggers thoughts of relaxation, sunny skies, warmth and happiness. If I say the word "classroom" that would elicit a completely different set of mental images. It's obvious that we form strong associations based on places, lighting, colors, and scents. Therefore, when considering how we want to present our Brand to the world it can be helpful to "borrow" from existing associations that might serve to strengthen our Brand.

Picture what a luxury spa looks like. If you're having trouble, just do an internet image search with the term "upscale spa." For the most part you'll see photos with clean, uncluttered spaces, neutral and warm colored walls and flooring, soothing lighting and well-appointed furniture. *That* - is what you're aiming for. It's these visuals that assist patients in making a decision as to whether or not to trust you with their face. Your office decor is a golden opportunity to reinforce the link between you and quality cosmetic treatment.

I think we can all agree that there's a pretty big difference between a Holiday Inn and a Ritz Carlton. When you walk into the lobby of either one, the design communicates the type of service and amenities you can expect. The furnishings, lighting and ambiance provide you with visual indicators of what type of experience the Brand aims to deliver. For instance, you wouldn't assume you'd find an expensive high-end restaurant at the Holiday Inn. On the other hand, you wouldn't be at all surprised if you walked into a Ritz Carlton and they were serving Afternoon Tea. Both hotel brands understand their target markets and work to create the experience their ideal consumer expects. Likewise, your office decor should help define an expectation.

I'm not advocating a full-on Windsor Castle motif. In fact, going over the top with opulence can backfire on you. Too much glitz might lead patients to assume your injectable fees are inflated to subsidize the lavish furnishings. In and of itself, that can be a barrier to entry. It's like that *"resort fee"* some hotels charge for all those "amenities" you never use but are still required to pay for. You need to find some middle ground. You might consider keeping the well-appointed furniture but ditch the massive Lenox crystal chandelier and the Faberge Egg tchotchkes. Ultimately, what you must do is create an atmosphere that allows patients to easily conclude that cosmetic services are a natural "fit" in your practice. Let's make this very plain. If you saw a well-known-chain high end steakhouse restaurant in the middle of a low-rent strip mall - wouldn't that give you pause? Wouldn't you doubt the food quality despite the name and logo on the sign? To put it another way, your workspace ambiance shouldn't be such that, a patient is shocked or skeptical when they find out your office provides cosmetic injectables.

This concept requires consideration well in advance of an injectable practice launch. Before you actively advertise your injectable practice it's important to look around the office with a fresh set of eyes. Try to see the spaces as your patients see them. Are they clean and organized? Is the furniture old and tatty? What kind of magazines are in the waiting room? Are they dog-eared and dated? Are they geared to your target audience or are they more suitable for another demographic?

A well designed, clean, orderly space provides an immediate visual statement to patients about how your office runs and how you work. It speaks directly about quality and efficiency. Everything matters in cosmetic practices and you have to earn trust at every touch point. Allowing yourself to believe that the skills and expertise you demonstrate in your present practice are so renowned that patients will flock to you for injectables is naive and reckless. Patients don't see it as a linear equation. You have to provide evidence of being worthy of the patients trust. Your workspace is an easy and logical place to begin with subtle but impactful cues that will help patients better understand the practice and its mission.

Don't assume you have to resort to the extreme. There's no need for Italian marble foyers and Boca Do Lobo furniture. Depending on your starting point you might not have to change much at all. But, be honest with yourself about the present condition of your office. Be sensible about what it might need and where you shop. There are plenty of options to purchase high quality furniture and decorator items at discounted prices.

Not everyone is born with impeccable design sense and it's nothing to be ashamed of. If you don't feel qualified to make decorating decisions, seek professional advice from someone who understands interior design - preferably not your spouse, unless your spouse is a bona fide interior decorator. You don't have to pay top dog for anything extravagant. Here are a few sites that won't break the budget: decorist.com, homepolish.com and havenly.com. They even offer online help options. If you're office already has good structure you might only need to change existing lighting or update other minor aspects. But you can't expect to grow an esthetic practice in a space that looks like you do root canals or drain abscesses all day. The visual incongruity is a strong barrier. For example, if your specialty is Ophthalmology, patients won't always make the natural connection between your training and facial esthetics. You need to build that bridge for them. If your office gives off more of a spa vibe than a medical-office-aura you facilitate that subliminal connection for the patient.

Don't forget about background shades of office walls and/or floors. Color is a significant element when making decisions about your Brand. Research published in the Journal of the Academy of Marketing Science suggests that color influences a customer's perception of a Brand's personality.[4] The psychology of color and its potential subliminal effects is a rich subject. If you're in the developmental stages of your Brand Identity, it's helpful to have a basic understanding of attitudes toward color and its influence on human behavior. Do an internet search with the term: "color psychology." That will give you a starting point especially when considering Brand development, logo design and/or office interior.

Just as a face changes with maturation, office decor shows signs of aging as well. Since we spend so much time in our offices, we usually don't see the fading features that make it look dated - it's the same as looking in the mirror every day - the transformation is too slow to be visible. Furniture doesn't come with an expiry date, so you have to use some common sense about its lifespan. If upholstery is wearing thin on chairs or the finish is rubbing off of the wood or laminate, it's time to change. If it looks soiled, I don't care how "comfortable" it is - get rid of it. Resist the pull of sentimentality. If you "can't part with that chair because it's been in the office since day one," enshrine it at home where your whole family can enjoy it. (see how long that lasts)

Think of how you want someone to feel when they walk into your office. Whatever those emotions are that you'd like to trigger, you

---

[4] Labrecque, L.I. & Milne, G.R. J. of the Acad. Mark. Sci. (2012) 40: 711. https://doi.org/10.1007/s11747-010-0245-y

have to provide cues to evoke those responses. To start on your way, write down all the words that describe the mood you want to create. Some examples might be luxury, safety, high-end, sophistication, exclusivity, welcoming, warmth, and privacy. Keep this list handy and before you commit to a decorator purchase, compare the item with the adjective, if they're not a match forget it and move on.

A cosmetic treatment room should be able to straddle the line between clinical and spa treatment. By this I mean it should be impeccably clean and have all the proper equipment - chair. lighting, sink, etc. Even though they're medical office favorites, please, eliminate the medical chart/illustration wall hangings. No one wants to stare at ear wax charts or multihued comparisons of pustules, vesicles and bullas while they're having dermal filler treatment. Wall decor should be consistent with the mood of the treatments, and therefore should be pleasing to the eye and depict traditional beauty. You can do this on a limited budget and don't have to invest in original art. Appropriate wall decorations can be found at sites like Wayfair.com and it's even possible to sort by size and genre when searching.

Good air circulation in treatment rooms is essential. If your treatment room doesn't dissipate heat well, or just for a matter of comfort, a quiet fan is really helpful. I keep one in each of my treatment rooms. It's nice to have even in the colder months when someone might be going vasovagal. I highly recommend the Rowenta VU2531 Turbo Silence Oscillating 12-Inch Table Fan - you can get it on Amazon at a good price and it really is quiet.

My experience has been that patients appreciate relaxing music during injectable treatments. How do I know this? Without prompting, patients often remark about how nice the background music is. An easy and inexpensive way to do this is by creating an 8 to 9-hour soundtrack on the computer in the treatment room. Since onboard sound devices are inexpensive to manufacture, most new PC's have integrated audio. Usually it's Windows Media Player, Groove or iTunes. So, unless you have an old computer running on legacy hardware, you should be able to play music. Once you've confirmed your computer's mp3 capability, just go to your favorite online digital music vendor and search for Spa Music albums. (another search term is: Relaxing Music) There are plenty of collections to choose from. Give them a listen to see which ones are to your liking. Most of these albums are fairly low-priced and have enough music for about an hour or two (or more!) of playing time - currently around $7 to $8. With a digital purchase, the music is immediately available. Be sure to get a pair of modestly priced speakers (available on Amazon) to make the audio quality of the music worth listening to, since internal computer speakers are usually lousy. Download the music directly to the computer (or transfer with a thumb drive), create a playlist and you're in business. (for a tutorial on setting up a playlist in Windows Media Player see footnote.[5]

In my office, staff turns on the music at the start of each day and it runs continuously - no commercials and no hassle.

---

[5] https://www.dummies.com/computers/operating-systems/windows-xp-vista/how-to-create-a-playlist-in-windows-media-player

Chapter 5

YOUR COSMETIC PRACTICE WARDROBE

"Good grooming is integral and impeccable style is a must. If you don't look the part, no one will want to give you time or money." Daymond John

What you wear, matters.[6] Sorry. Much like a patient's initial impression is made when walking into your reception area, your attire is a major visual by which people form an opinion of you. In fact, research tells us that first impressions are made within 7 seconds of meeting someone.[7] Despite rabid objections from well-intentioned people claiming we should base our judgements solely on character, humans seem to be hardwired to form initial personality assessments based on appearance. Society as a whole is visually based, and clothing provides powerful social signals, even if those signals are unfounded. Especially in the cosmetic practice realm, patients use all their senses to make judgements on a practitioner's attention to detail.

---

[6] https://www.washingtonpost.com/posteverything/wp/2015/07/07/forget-scrubs-doctors-need-a-dress-code/?noredirect=on
[7] https://www.forbes.com/sites/serenitygibbons/2018/06/19/you-have-7-seconds-to-make-a-first-impression-heres-how-to-succeed/#5f88064356c2

In the time it takes to shake hands and introduce yourself, even before you have a chance to utter anything scholarly or eloquent, a prospective patient has made a quick judgement on your clinical experience and skills. Yes, it's wholly unfair. But, with an abundance of research clearly demonstrating this fact, we're foolish to ignore it.[8] Moreover, knowing that personal style and clothing is one of the first exposures someone has to your Brand, why not take full advantage of it? As esthetic practitioners we have much to prove before a patient will trust their face in our hands - if you want to play the role you have to look the part.

Long before I started my injectable practice, I was in the habit of wearing business attire under a crisp white lab coat. To me, a white lab coat is a statement accessory and studies indicate that most patients prefer it too.[9] Unless you're a general surgeon, scrubs are less commanding and don't declare authority. They convey a more casual and less serious message. Since they're worn by every level of personnel from janitor up to the most senior doctor, they no longer differentiate position or authority. Sure, they're an easy wardrobe option, but in my opinion, in the cosmetic practice scrubs are best left to support staff.

Personal grooming is an easy parameter to control. You don't have to look like Angelina Jolie or Brad Pitt, but you must present the best version of yourself every day. This includes teeth, hair and nails. In the era of over-the-counter teeth whitening strips there's no reason

---

[8] https://www.emerald.com/insight/content/doi/10.1108/13612021311305128/full/html
[9] https://labblog.uofmhealth.org/rounds/what-doctors-wear-really-does-matter-to-patients

to have dark and discolored teeth. (yes, they work, trust me I'm a dentist) Purchase them, use them and repeat them often.

Gray hair roots practically scream inattention to detail. I personally resent nearly every moment I have to spend at the Hairdresser and have been coloring my own hair - practically since Reagan was president. I've eliminated hundreds of hours (and thousands of dollars) spent in the salon and I can be fully productive in my home during those 45 minutes needed for the color to work. I'm not advocating that you color your own hair, but you should make it a priority to schedule a standing appointment every 3-4 weeks to keep those roots out of sight. In addition to sloppiness, gray roots also suggest neglect, poverty and indifference. At the level of healthcare practitioner, allowing something so easily corrected to define you, is inexcusable.

Often called the "body's business card," hands are another criterion used to make judgments about you. Admittedly, men don't often pay attention to other men's paws - but women do. Especially during a consultation when you might be pointing to the computer or anything else. Yes, We Are Looking. Much like a smooth face with a clear complexion, well-groomed nails and smooth hands speak volumes about their owner. Although not entirely new, male mani's have become more mainstream, with gentlemen-targeted spas cropping up everywhere. You might think this is a Millennial-thing, but the truth is male executives and professionals have long understood the importance of elegant looking hands. Professional manicures are not compulsory, but your nails should be clean, shaped and buffed and your hands should appear soft and smooth.

AND FOR FEMALES:

Sorry, chipped nail polish is not a trend I can get behind. If you don't have the time, inclination or interest in having perfectly polished nails - don't do it at all. It's much better to have clean, trimmed and unpainted nails than laying bare, with tatty nails in varying degrees of chipped polish. Since well-manicured nails take time and money to maintain they're viewed as a high-end accessory. Flawlessly polished nails indicate an investment in appearance which is interpreted as fastidious and conscientious. These are definitely the qualities sought after in a cosmetic practitioner. Unfortunately, tatty nails, like so many other things in life - look worse on older individuals. A banged-up manicure on the mature individual not only looks unkempt but also implies "financially unsuccessful." Gel nail polish is more expensive but basically eliminates chipped and tatty looking nails.

Chapter 6

OVERHEAD CONTROL

"Take care of the pennies and the pounds will take care of themselves" English proverb

One of the biggest advantages existing practice owners have when adding injectable treatments is, they probably already own all or most of the major equipment that's needed. Unlike Coolsculpting, Fraxel or Laser Tattoo removal, injectables have no major up-front equipment costs. With few exceptions, if your practice involves seeing patients you have at least one treatment chair. And chances are you probably have a good light source and a small refrigerator. Fortunately, that's really all you need to get started. I strongly advise against making any major purchases and sinking a ton of cash into specialized equipment until the injectable practice is up and running. Despite the excitement and joy that comes with brand-new equipment, in the early stages you should funnel resources into things that matter, such as additional education and training. Specialized lighting and pretty furniture won't make you a better injector.

For the first 6 years of my injectable practice I treated patients while they were seated in a dental chair with an overhead dental light. Although sufficient, I was never entirely happy with the limitations of the light. It was plenty bright but only capable of illuminating a small rectangular area measuring about 8 by 4 inches. Everything outside of that rectangle looked dark in contrast to the illuminated area. During treatment I was constantly adjusting its position to make sure the treatment area had enough light. I knew at some point I wanted to replace it with something better - something that would cast light on the entire face. Another annoyance was the small sink that attaches to one side of the dental chair. I like to stand on the treatment side of the patients face (right or left) when placing dermal fillers. The sink made it awkward and limited my access to the left side of the patient. None of these inconveniences impacted my ability to deliver quality treatment but they did affect my time efficiency - and my mood.

One day I walked into treatment room 4 and it dawned on me that I hadn't done any dental procedures in there for over four years. I knew it was time to upgrade. At that point I ditched all the dental equipment, placed a derm chair and had an LED derm light installed. The light was purchased from an online supplier. I asked for a discount - and I got one. It wasn't huge, but I didn't pay the list price. I purchased the chair from a used equipment supplier and opted for upgraded leather. I was able to match the color of the other chairs in my treatment suites - avoiding the mismatched hodge-podge look. Refurbished chairs are far less expensive and usually come with a small but serviceable warranty. I added a refrigerator and a functional but stylish cabinet, set up a permanent area for photo-documentation and never looked back. The refrigerator may seem like an indulgence but for me it's indispensable. I'm one of those crazy lunatics that goes ballistic if I see a reconstituted bottle of Botox out on the counter for more than 5 minutes. Since the refrigerator is right below the counter, I can personally ensure that the bottle is safely returned to its sanctuary as soon as I'm done with it.

At the start of my injectable practice I didn't have a backlog of people queued up at the door. I have a small boutique office with zero inclination for overhead excess. So, keeping a large inventory is not something I've ever done. From an economic perspective the supplies needed for an injectable practice have minimal financial impact. I've read articles authored by doctors who claim that injectable practice startup expenses are high. This is completely false. Either they don't know the actual cost of supplies or they're just parroting something they read somewhere else. Needles, syringes, saline, lidocaine and alcohol preps are the very basics - and they are dirt cheap. Blunt end cannula and chlorhexidine wipes are slightly more expensive, but you don't need massive quantities - especially when you first start out. The most expensive items are the injectable products themselves (Botox®, Juvederm®, Restylane®, etc.) and there's no reason whatsoever to keep them in large supply.

When it comes to stocking the actual injectable products (neurotoxins and dermal fillers) I recommend keeping very limited supplies on hand until your injectable practice is really humming. Don't let sales reps talk you into buying multiple types of dermal fillers because of the "on label" indications or because you get a better deal when you buy in bulk. It's not a "good deal" if you wind up throwing it away when it expires. And remember, for many years the only product on the market was Restylane. We treated everything with it back then and it still remains one of the mainstays in the world of fillers. There's no law that restricts you from using a product outside the areas of its FDA approval when there's science to back it up. For instance, when treating the malar area, you don't have to exclusively use Voluma simply because it has FDA approval for that indication. You can choose to use products in off-label areas provided they are well-suited for that application and supported by scientific literature.

It bears repeating that in the early phases of your injectable practice, minimizing the number of products you keep on hand is a smart way to limit overhead costs. It also minimizes the risk of having expensive products sitting in a drawer beyond their expiration date. I didn't stock every FDA approved product until my injectable practice really took off. In the beginning, I kept a maximum of 4 syringes on hand at any given time. This meant my only hyaluronic acid dermal filler products were from Allergan. This wasn't because I felt they were superior - all FDA approved products have their merits - it's because when purchasing from Allergan I wasn't on the hook for a large minimum order. At the time this book is being written, Galderma - the distributor of the Restylane product line, has a minimum order of six syringes. For a small boutique practice, tying up that kind of capital in products that you might not need for several months is difficult and foolish. Moreover, if the product reaches its expiration date you can't exchange it for a non-expired replacement. It then becomes a financial loss.

Allergan dispenses their dermal filler products in boxes of two syringes. So, two boxes contain four syringes. In addition to the supreme advantage of "no minimum order," Allergan's delivery is spot-on reliable. If you place your order today - unless today is Friday - your order arrives tomorrow. This means, if you know you have a patient coming in on Wednesday, if you order on Monday, you'll have your product the day before your patient is scheduled. With the current Allergan business model there's really no need to keep large inventories. I think this Allergan marketing strategy is pretty darn smart. They position their products to establish brand loyalty at an early phase in the injectors practice. The same holds true with Botox. For the developing injectable practice this takes a lot of financial heat off of inventory management.

While we're on the subject of neurotoxins (Botox), even though it's perfectly acceptable to use the same vial for more than one patient, the Center for Disease Control (CDC) states that it's unacceptable to use multi-dose vials beyond 28 days after opening.[10] This is true for saline and lidocaine as well. The rationale behind this is that preservatives may break down and compromise sterility allowing for bacterial growth within the vial. Please note that if you decide to use non-preserved saline for reconstitution you have to discard the vial after 24 hours.[11]

Whenever you open a vial of anything, write the date on the label. Don't ever risk causing a bacterial infection in a patient's face because you were either careless or too cheap to discard the unused product after 28 days. *Primum non nocere!* It's not a gamble worth taking and it's patently wrong. This is why, when I first began my injectable practice, I only purchased 50-unit bottles of Botox - I found it much less painful to potentially discard 10-15 units of Botox than it would have been to discard 40 or 50 units. Yes, it's true that 50-unit bottles are slightly more expensive per unit, but it's well worth it. In those early days of my injectable practice, I was treating maybe 2 to 4 patients a month with Botox. At that rate there was no doubt that I would have been discarding unused units at the end of 28-day cycles.

Once your injectable practice is up and running, you'll need to stock the expensive injectables in greater supply. Be certain this segment of your inventory grows proportional to - and doesn't exceed - expected needs. Again, don't fall prey to advertised specials from

---

[10] https://www.cdc.gov/injectionsafety/providers/provider_faqs_multivials.html
[11] https://www.botoxmedical.com/Common/Assets/APC15WD15_Recon_Dilution_Instructions.pdf

the distributors. Only keep on hand what you reasonably predict should be used within 3 to 4 months.

OTHER ITEMS AND SUPPLIES

Don't feel obliged to order common disposable items from your usual supply house. I've found that the big-name vendors have big time markups on products that can be purchased elsewhere for less. I don't buy any of my syringes or needles from the Big-Names. {For my latest list of product vendors go here: **bit.ly/PracticeForms**} Just because I'm frugal doesn't mean I disregard quality. I'm finicky about needles and I've identified some direct to consumer warehouses that have great prices for the same name-brands offered by medical suppliers. However, when you're purchasing saline or lidocaine make sure you're buying from a reputable dealer and the products are intended for human use - not veterinarian supply. Alcohol preps are the same no matter where you get them, so why spend more than you have to?

Let's talk a little bit about your refrigerator. I mentioned that at a certain point I changed out the equipment in a treatment room since I no longer did dentistry in it. By this time my injectable practice was up and running and I had to stock a larger inventory of products. Aside from allowing easy access to the biologics, it ensured the Botox went right into the fridge after I treated a patient. But no matter where your refrigerator is, here's some strong advice - if you keep expensive products in it, buy a refrigerator thermometer with an alarm. Trust me on this one. When I revamped the treatment room I foolishly "upgraded" to a fancy name-brand refrigerator. Within a short span of time, perhaps four months we returned after a weekend to find the refrigerator was at room temperature - but the light inside it was still functioning. There was no way of knowing when the unit failed so the contents had to be considered compromised and couldn't be used. Suffice it to say, the amount of product I had in the refrigerator when it failed was equal to the cost of a very nice automobile. I immediately went back to the cheaper model refrigerator. I'd had nearly 20 years' experience with the less fancy fridge and it never failed me. For half the price, I replaced the Gourmet Fridge with the old brand and immediately placed an alarm inside it. I purchased the device from Amazon for about $150 dollars. It wirelessly connects to my phone via a free app. I can check the temperature and humidity any time day or night. I set the temperature parameters and it sends me a text if the limits are exceeded. After that calamitous experience, I consider the alarm to be an essential piece of equipment in an injectable practice.

If you're using hyaluronic acid based dermal fillers, you absolutely must keep a stash of hyaluronidase. If you've already completed training, you know that hyaluronidase is the HA filler dissolver. It's an essential item and it's the standard of care to both have it and know how to use it when necessary. At the time of this book writing, the recommendation is to have approximately 3-4 thousand units on hand. The product is supplied in 150-unit vials sold in boxes of four. (600 units total) You need to have about 7 boxes on hand (28 vials total). At current prices, each box of 4 vials is several hundred dollars. Since all pharmaceuticals carry an expiration date, rather than have one month when all the hyaluronidase expires and needs replacement here's how we do it: We purchase one new box every other month in odd numbered months. (you might decide to order in even numbered months - your choice) My staff knows they need to order a new box January, March, May, etc. and this continues throughout the year in all odd numbered months. As the orders arrive, staff knows to find the box that's expiring and throws it away.

Having a rotation like this saves you from the hair-raising experience of reaching in the fridge for the Hylenex only to find that every single vial is expired. It also eases the financial burden of having to replace the entire supply once a year - to the tune of a few thousand dollars.

Here's a list of the major equipment you'll need to get started in injectables:

Treatment Room
Treatment Chair
Good Lighting
Refrigerator
Storage Space
Area with consistent lighting for Photodocumentation
Camera
Refrigerator thermometer with alarm
Secure Software to store photos

Remember, there's no sense in changing out your existing treatment chair or lighting unless they are tatty and old, until your injectable practice has really blossomed and consuming space on a regular basis. Personally, I may have waited a bit longer than I should have but it didn't have any adverse effects on the treatment delivery or practice growth.

Chapter 7

GRAY MARKET PRODUCTS

"Follow the rules or follow the fools." Tupac Shakur

Where there's money to be made there's potential for illegal activity and the cosmetic injectable market is no exception. Whatever you do, DO NOT be tempted by unauthorized (Gray Market) purveyors of regulated products. Let me explain: Gray Markets are unofficial businesses that operate outside of authorized distribution networks. They supply products to anyone willing to purchase them. These products can be either counterfeit pharmaceuticals or a product that has exited the legitimate pipeline and is now sold by an unauthorized seller. The problems with each of these are as follows:

1. A counterfeit product can be a substitute product (even something that's potentially harmful) or it can be the actual product but in an unknown quantity. The quantity is usually lower as a result of being cut or reduced for redistribution and masquerading as the full-strength product.

2. Legitimate product that's resold by an illegitimate distributor is problematic and potentially harmful due to lack of oversight of its care and handling once it leaves the authorized distributor. These products may be subject to wide temperature variations or other

mishandling that may compromise sterility or effect. It's impossible to know anything about the product's movements through the pirated system or what conditions it's been subjected to.

Regardless of which breach we're talking about, Gray Market Products are considered unsafe for patient use and can absolutely land you in hot water.[12] If you inject a patient with these products and a problem results, the legitimate distributor is not liable for any damages. You stand alone in defending yourself from the indefensible. The risks associated with using pharmaceuticals considered "Gray Market," completely outstrip any small savings you might realize by using such products - not to mention that it's ILLEGAL. A few years ago, I had a great conversation with one of my reps about Gray Market Products. He told me this: "Gigi, I get the same Groupon notifications that everyone else does. When I see the name of a practice or doctor on a Groupon offer that I don't recognize, I look them up. If the practice is in my territory, I immediately know if they have an account with us. If they don't, and they're advertising my company's product, I know it has to be Gray Market. It's that simple."

The bottom line is this, don't let greed or ignorance entice you into making bad decisions. Never purchase products from anyone other than the authorized distributor. Products sold in the Gray Market, no matter where the product started, are considered non-FDA approved.

---

[12] https://www.fda.gov/inspections-compliance-enforcement-and-criminal-investigations/press-releases/november-10-2016-nurse-who-operated-spa-laguna-niguel-agrees-plead-guilty-illegally-dispensing-botox

Chapter 8

CREATING YOUR FEE SCHEDULE

"Charge what you're worth and don't apologise."
Chris Ducker

An important and practical business consideration is how to structure your injectable fees. This requires careful thought and it's not as simple as calculating how much you'd like to earn per hour. The fees you charge should be competitive in your geographic market, incorporate overhead costs and reflect your level of training and expertise. Geographic market and overhead costs should be easy to quantify, so we won't discuss them here. Let's take a closer look at how training affects your fee since it's not a simple math calculation like overhead and not an economic factor like geographic segmentation.

It's an established fact that most specialists charge higher fees than generalists for many of the exact same procedures. In many cases, this is appropriate given the level of formal advanced training specialists undergo. Further, the procedures that specialists charge a premium for are not delegable to extenders or mid-level providers. Since most states allow injectables to be delegated, it would seem logical that those fees shouldn't be subject to a premium in the case where a specialist is the treating practitioner. For example, when an

RN injects patients with Botox or dermal fillers at a plastic surgeon's office, it would be extremely rare (almost unheard of) that the fee charged for that procedure would be less than if the plastic surgeon did the injections.

There's a wide range of practitioners across the US and other Countries who can, according to their licenses, administer facial injectables. As mentioned, a key determinant of the fee charged is the level of skill, expertise and specific injectable education. In the field of injectables, these factors supersede whatever your core specialty may or may not be. For instance, I know that in my geographic location there are core specialists who don't pursue yearly training in injectables. This field is very young and continues to evolve. If you don't make it your business to learn the latest breakthroughs, techniques and standards you'll certainly be left behind in very short order. Accordingly, the fees you charge should reflect your fidelity to continuing education.

I strongly advise against using low fees as a practice builder. To find out what other practices are charging, do what they do - block your phone number and call them and ask what they charge for "X" procedure. Many offices won't quote fee's over the phone - and with good reason. You shouldn't allow your staff to quote fees either. Patients and clinicians rarely speak the same language and most individuals don't have medical training that would allow them to understand how many units of neurotoxin or how many syringes of dermal filler they might need. In spite of this obvious knowledge gap, some offices will quote fees over the phone. When they do, you can use this information to evaluate your market and where you might want to position yourself. Generally, when starting out, you don't want to be at the top or the bottom. Somewhere in-between is a good place to begin. As my front desk manager has told me: you can always go up - but going down looks very bad.

I'll never understand why, but there's an unending supply of offices that advertise injectables with Groupon. Let me explain the inherent problems with "Social Coupons" such as Groupon, for health care practitioners. First, you should know that Groupon is a "fee splitting" arrangement whereby, in exchange for advertising, the Seller (in this case - the practice) keeps half the profits and Groupon receives the other half. The vital element here is that most, if not all Medical and Dental Organizations (including AMA[13], ASAPS[14], ADA[15]) have statements within their code of ethics that declare Fee-Splitting as unethical. Moreover, in many states, using social coupons in medicine/dentistry is considered illegal. An entire conversation about fee-splitting goes beyond the scope of this book but suffice it to say that most states have laws concerning this concept. The main purpose of these regulations is to prevent kickbacks to third parties for promoting medical services.

In addition to its briery ethical and legal complexion, Social Coupons are no way to build an injectable practice. The type of person attracted by a low price point for facial injectables from an unknown practitioner is loyal to no one. These are opportunistic practice hoppers - they look for deals and don't give a fig about quality. Moreover, when you're lowering your price (Groupon requires that it be at least 50% lower than your usual fee) and then forking over half of that bare-bones sum to the Social Coupon advertising platform, the question becomes how much is the ad scheme costing you and is

---

[13] https://www.ama-assn.org/delivering-care/ethics/fee-splitting 11.3.4
[14] https://www.surgery.org/sites/default/files/ASAPS-Code-of-Ethics.pdf, 3.03
[15] http://www.ada.org/~/media/ADA/Publications/Files/ADA_Code_of_Ethics_2018.pdf?la=en 5.Γ.4

the juice worth the squeeze? You're betting on being able to retain that patient long-term, a risky wager with no data to support it. Social Coupons are and should be viewed only as advertising. Instead of paying up-front to place an ad online or in print you "amortize" the cost by losing money when treating those patients. The other thing Social Coupons do is make your practice look desperate. When existing patients see these ads, it can create the perception that your normal fees are too high. Using Groupon to drive new patients to your office is not only highly offensive to your existing loyal patients but forces you to recover those losses at their expense, which flies in the face of good business practice.

Bottom line? Social Coupons are unethical, potentially illegal, disrespectful to full paying practice members and economically reckless.

Chapter 9

SCHEDULING INJECTABLE PATIENTS

"There are no shortcuts to any place worth going."
Beverly Sills

Appointment scheduling and time allocation are among the most common questions I'm asked when I teach. Most new injectors want to know how much time each procedure is expected to take and how to integrate these treatments into their existing schedules. When I first started doing injectables the amount of time I allotted was naturally, much more than it is now. If you're like most practitioners, the same will be true for you. This is one of the reasons why treating your employees can be helpful. (more on this later) Like any procedure you do in your office it takes a few rounds before you and your staff feels comfortable and have an established routine in place. These procedural patterns promote quality treatment. I strongly urge you to create systems for every procedure you do. When you follow a step-by-step agenda, it becomes less likely that you'll omit anything. You think it won't happen but, trust me, it will if you and your staff don't have a well-defined game plan.

Every practice has its own unique daily interruptions and distractions. Most of these intrusions are part and parcel to the nature of the business's focus and have minimal impact on the flow of normal office activity. However, some interruptions are capable of completely derailing your train of thought. Instituting a policy of no interruptions during procedures can help, but rules always have exceptions and in medicine some things just cannot wait. Even casual banter with the patient you're treating can allow you to momentarily *lose your place* in the treatment sequence. This is why having a set Playbill is so important. Systems create efficiency and serve to remind you and your staff of the next step in the process. Generally speaking, there are four enemies of consistent quality. They are distraction, haste, complacency and laziness. Distraction usually comes from external forces whereas the other three are a matter of attitude and personal discipline. Establishing systems for office procedures is a way to gain control over efficiency and quality.

I'll share a few of the systems we use in my office to demonstrate what I mean. You can take these and modify to your liking.

Unless there's a consultation at the visit, here is my basic system for:

NEUROMODULATORS:

- **Patient seated**
- **Photodocumentation**
- **Consent signed**
- **Face cleansed**
- Affirmation of treatment areas with patient
- Diagnostic markings
- Pull up volumes
- Inject

- Post op instructions

AND FOR DERMAL FILLERS:

- **Patient seated**
- **Photodocumentation**
- **Consent signed**
- **Face cleansed**
- Affirmation of treatment areas
- Skin prep with antimicrobial wipes
- Lidocaine administration
- Injections
- Post op instructions
- Final photodocumentation

AND FOR KYBELLA (DEOXYCHOLIC ACID):

- **Patient seated**
- **Photodocumentation**
- **Consent signed**
- **Patient draped**
- **Neck cleaned**
- Patient marked
- Grid placed
- Unnecessary Grid dots removed
- Pre-treatment Ice applied
- Deoxycholic acid drawn up in syringes
- Patient injected
- Ice applied immediately and grid dots removed

- Post op instructions

The steps in bold print are completed by my nurse/assistant. All other items are completed by me.

As I mentioned, in the early days of my injectable practice I was slower and required more time to consider my treatment plan and inject. At that stage I'd schedule about 30 minutes on my active (main) schedule for neuromodulators. Once I became more experienced and confident, I moved neurotoxin treatments to my non-active (emergency) schedule. Here's how we do it: Much of the prep is done by my nurse and depending on how much time I spend talking and "socializing" with my patient, my part takes only about 5-15 minutes. While I'm with the Botox patient, there's another patient in separate treatment room, either waiting for local anesthesia to take effect or having an x-ray taken, being triaged, etc. - you get the picture.

I'm fortunate that my front desk manager happens to have amazing business acumen. Her parents owned a shoe store when she was growing up and she clearly learned and understood good business practices. I credit a large amount of my injectable practice growth to her and what she's taught me. Once I started placing Botox patients on my non-active schedule, she began scheduling in a way that I didn't immediately have an appreciation for. She explained to me that "Botox is a want." When a patient calls to set up a Botox appointment she moved heaven and earth to get them in that day. She said, "they want it - and they don't want to wait for it. We should get them in today on our schedule before they call another office." Her method was right on the mark. Cosmetic treatment is very unlike my core specialty of dentistry. Most people would put off garden-variety dental treatment for any reason. The only exception is cosmetic dentistry, which goes to prove the point.

Generally speaking, when the focus of medical or dental treatment is not cosmetic, most patients value a practitioner who 1) sees them on time and 2) doesn't keep them in the office forever. When I started my injectable practice, I was naive. I assumed injectable patients were no different from other patients. Little did I know that cosmetic patients had different expectations from their practitioner and were much more tolerant, perhaps even indulgent, in the time spent in the treatment chair. It was transformative for me and my practice when I realized this.

Before this epiphany, I moved as quickly as I could through the procedure without compromising safety, racing to the finish. Looking back now I'd say my results at that time were good, but not over-the-top good. Then, I'm not sure why, but one day before starting the next dermal filler case I decided to slow everything down. I'd inject, back-up and evaluate the patient from the anterior view, the lateral view, coronal view, and take the time to look at the effect I was having before adding more or moving to another area. I definitely find that the coronal view (standing behind the patient chair and looking down from the top of the head) is really helpful when evaluating symmetry. I noticed my end results improved as I slowed down and took the time to assess my progress. Quite unexpectedly, my patients seemed to appreciate the slower, more thoughtful approach as well. Without prompting, some patients would offer that their prior injector(s) didn't evaluate their face or the progress during their treatment as I did. It was clear from their comments and their tone that they valued the slower, more deliberate approach. To my surprise, I also found that I was enjoying doing dermal fillers like never before. My results began to look so much more elegant and on target. Once I realized this I never looked back. I was using product more judiciously and the reaction from my patients clearly demonstrated that they appreciated a more intentional and precise approach.

Facial cosmetic treatments allow no room for error. Especially when first getting started, don't skimp on appointment time allocation. Be assured that your "speed" will increase with experience. Patients are grateful for your time and devotion to excellence. Moreover, their face becomes your billboard for advertisement.

Chapter 10

DISCOUNTS

"Repeat business or behavior can be bribed. Loyalty has to be earned." Janet L. Robinson

I don't believe anyone who says they "never" discount. Maybe *now* they don't discount, but there was a time when they did - perhaps they called it something else and that made them feel better. But when you're working to start an injectable practice (or any business), there are a lot of things you'll do to create loyal, happy patient ambassadors. Like other marketing strategies, the secret to using discounts is knowing when and who should receive them. There's nothing wrong with offering an occasional complementary treatment or product to someone who's been a loyal patient of record and has had multiple procedures in your office. Likewise, if someone has sent multiple good patients to you, it's appropriate to reward them in some way. Apart from the discount, it's important that these valued members of your practice know <u>why</u> they're receiving it. Your team should understand this and bring it to the patients' attention. For example, at the point of payment your receptionist might say, "Mrs. Doe, as a thanks for the kind referral you recently sent to us, you'll notice there's a discount on your bill today. Our practice relies heavily on word of mouth and we greatly appreciate referrals."

Whenever possible, I urge you to avoid discounting fees for new patients of the practice. For example, let's say a new patient you treated with Botox returns for the 2 week follow up and you need to add units to correct something minor, like a Mephisto sign. If you're charging by the unit, which I highly recommend, patients will and should expect to pay for the extra units needed. If they call again in yet another 2 weeks, unhappy with something else, RESIST the urge to try to quiet them down by adding a few Botox units for free. The correct thing to do at this juncture is to tell them they need to wait for the (scientifically based and recommended) 3-month period for retreatment. Believe me when I tell you, if you allow the squeaky wheel to demand the free grease, there will be no end to it. Until you have a proven history with a loyal patient, and they establish an unblemished record free of bellyaching, I would absolutely avoid any freebies with them. This type of character will drive your entire staff crazy and occupy too much space in your head to make even one free unit worthwhile.

Depending on which study you read, the cost of recruiting a new patient can be anywhere between 5 and 25% more expensive than retaining an existing one. Clearly, keeping your existing base happy is a financially solid investment.

Chapter 11

TREATING YOUR STAFF

"If you take care of your employees, they will take care of the clients." Richard Branson

Without a doubt, there are definite advantages to providing injectable treatments for your staff. But let's be honest, not all staff are created equal. When it comes to treating employees, you have to apply the same criteria you use for screening regular, garden variety, paying patients. And to complicate matters further, saying "no" to the people you work side by side with every day requires a lot more delicacy than saying "no" to patients you see only occasionally. Here's the tightrope that you have to walk: On the one hand, you risk pissing off an otherwise valued employee by refusing to treat them. They could wind up feeling spurned, especially if they know you've treated other staff members. Then, on the other hand, you don't want to feel like you're on the hook for a zillion Botox and/or filler revisions, trying in vain to please someone who's downright impossible to satisfy. Anywhere you find yourself along this continuum of unpleasant terrain is a tough place to be. Always think it through before committing to treating anyone. A while ago I wrote an article on how to recognize poor injectable candidates and how to say "no." For more information and deeper explanation on that subject you can find it here: http://bit.ly/ShouldYouTreat

Just like the rest of us, after attending training sessions, staff will usually identify potential areas for correction on themselves. In fact, even before you commit to training, they may offer or "suggest" their willingness to be a model patient for you. Thankfully most people, including staff, are generally acceptable injectable candidates. Treating your staff can be a smart business decision, provided you establish rational parameters before you pick up the syringe. And for better or for worse - treating employees with facial injectables can be the most effective staff retention program you'll ever institute.

Let's explore why establishing game rules is so important. Here's an example: Let's say you're a medical practitioner, and a staff member (for whatever reason) would like to have blood drawn every 3 months or so to test a certain lab value. For the sake of argument, we'll assume there's no underlying health issue that would require these tests and therefore would not be covered by insurance. In this scenario, would you not charge that staff person the lab fee? Here's another example if you're a dentist: if a staff member needed to have a crown replaced on the same tooth, every 3 months, would you not charge them the lab fee?? I hope you answered "yes' to these hypothetical questions. Remember this: injectables are the gift that keeps on giving. With few exceptions, they're usually not a "one-off' event and patients ordinarily require regular maintenance. With neurotoxins, that would be every 3-4 months. With dermal fillers, it might be anywhere from every 6 to 18 months. And remember, you supply (pay for) the product.

Here's how we do it in my office: the staff understands that they pay **my cost** for injectables. The only time this rule is suspended is at the end of the year - during the holiday season. In addition to any financial bonus that might be given, they receive whatever injectables they might desire - either Botox or Filler - in some cases both. If you have a sizable staff and even if you don't, the costs associated with giving product away on a monthly basis could amount to multiple thousands every year. That's something you need to think through BEFORE you treat your staff. Establish the ground rules with your team as soon as you decide to add injectables to your practice. Create a document that clearly spells out everything so there's no misunderstanding. If an employee expresses interest in injectables, have the office manager give them a copy before any appointments are made. That's much easier than having to deliver the sorry news after the fact.

Apart from potentially creating a more beautiful, loyal and contented team, other practice benefits can be had by treating your staff. To fully appreciate this, we need to return our focus to injectable patients and take a look at their behavior. Regular consumers of facial injectables develop traits similar to car enthusiasts. What do I mean by that? With both car enthusiasts and regular injectable patients, you can say this: Their interest leads them to become passionate observers. They know a lot about current trends and technology and which features (products) deliver the best bang for the buck. They're also discerning critics and know when modifications have been made.

How does this fit in our conversation about the benefits of treating staff? Any of your existing patients who have had injectables (and even some who might be considering injectables) will likely notice the injectable transformations in your staff. And as your skills grow and improve, so will the results on the faces of your staff. Even the most subtle changes can spark interest. I'm often stunned at how bold patients can be. They're entirely unafraid to flat-out ask my staff what they recently had done. We've had women walk up to my front desk person and say, "whatever she did to you, I want that done!" This has been an amazing injectable practice builder as well as an unexpected and successful patient recruitment tool.

Remember, you need to apply the same patient assessment criteria to staff. If you feel a staff member has unrealistic expectations, body dysmorphia or potential family disapproval, you have to consider not treating them. This is a difficult situation and requires very delicate handling. Since the focus of this book is growing your injectable practice and not employee management or body dysmorphia, we'll stay within the scope of our objective.

Chapter 12

CONSULTATION AND PATIENT SELECTION

"The single biggest problem in communication is the illusion that it has taken place." George Bernard Shaw

Treating the esthetic patient is not like treating a patient who is sick or injured. In its most basic form - it's the difference between a "want" and a "need." Unfortunately, most training courses provide little if any guidance when it comes to cosmetic patient selection. It's true that treatment in the esthetic realm exposes the practitioner to risks not inherent for non-esthetic practitioners. Identifying those individuals who are poor candidates for esthetic treatment can be difficult and often relies on the practitioners innate "spidey-senses." We'll discuss some of the established guidelines, but to be perfectly frank, gut-instinct is probably correct more often than it's wrong. When in doubt - refer it out. You'll never regret the patient you didn't treat.

Assessing a patient's needs and determining if appropriate treatment includes injectables is only a small part of the patient selection process. One of the key indicators that helps determine whether the doctor-patient relationship should continue is *rapport*. What I'm really saying is: "Are you and the patient compatible?" As we've all experienced, there are times when compatibility (or incompatibility) is obvious from the moment you walk into the room. But in most cases, recognizing the practitioner-patient "fit" takes more time and requires a bit of dialogue. Verbal communication is the primary means by which the patient and practitioner exchange information and develop a rapport. If at the end of the consultation, you don't feel like you're in alignment with the patient or if you don't like them, don't treat them.

WATCH YOUR LANGUAGE

Every segment of medicine has its unique vocabulary. Some might call it jargon. Most of us have honed our ability to communicate medical/dental terms and phrases to make them understandable to our patients. This is absolutely critical when discussing diagnosis or treatment options. Likewise, we need to develop those same skills when talking about injectables. Using unfamiliar industry language with patients creates a communication barrier. For me, I liken this to my interactions with my IT people. Yes, I understand a lot of the tech industry buzzwords, but when they start talking to me about what my office needs for the next upgrade and they throw out those first two or three techie terms I'm usually lost. Moreover, I'm reluctant to ask them to explain each foreign concept since this could make a 45-minute discussion devolve into a two-hour symposium. So, I wind up trying to figure out what they're talking about by drawing inferences from context and nodding my head, so I don't look completely daft. Since I only understand half (okay, less than half) of what they're saying, no matter what they recommend, I usually end up feeling cheated or duped. It would be a gigantic benefit to their profession, if IT people would eliminate their industry jargon when speaking to their customers. But since this hasn't been my experience, my jaded assessment is that I'm being swindled. Rationally, I know this is probably not the case 100% of the time, but I'm suspicious none-the-less. Anyway, I imagine this is how patients feel when they don't understand our language. Rather than making the practitioner sound "smart," speaking in industry jargon can give patients the impression they're being bamboozled or upsold.

Successful cosmetic treatment of any kind, ultimately relies primarily on the patients satisfaction. To that end, a patient's ability to convey their desired outcome is at the very heart of where we need to begin. And let's be honest, patients are also guilty of having their own language that we as practitioners don't understand. They usually choose words and descriptors that are completely alien to us and to make matters worse they frequently use medical terms incorrectly. When this happens don't get hung up on semantics; be the bigger person and resist the desire to "school" the patient in correct medical terminology. Instead, patiently drill down to uncover the genuine meaning the individual is trying to convey. Likewise, when communicating with patients, it's best to use the clear term, even when you know it's not the perfect term.

Here's an example of how a patient can use a verbal description that could lead to a misdiagnosis: A fairly common event after upper face treatment with neurotoxin is brow ptosis. This results from over-medicating the Frontalis muscle. As a byproduct of its primary function of raising the eyebrows, Frontalis also pulls the skin up and away from the eyes. Therefore, in addition to a lower brow position, decreased contractility in this muscle can give the appearance of heavy eyelids. Being unfamiliar with facial muscles and anatomy, a patient experiencing brow ptosis may call the office and say that their "eyelids are drooping." Educated injectors know that eyelid ptosis (drooping eyelids) is a completely different problem with an entirely separate etiology from brow ptosis. Moreover, each of these clinical presentations are dealt with in wholly unrelated ways. Unlike brow ptosis, true eyelid ptosis can't be alleviated with the addition of neurotoxin in the brow depressors. In fact, eyelid ptosis can only be treated palliatively - if it's treated at all. The bottom line is, you can't rely on a patient's description of a problem and expect to make an accurate diagnosis. You have to see them in person.

I've learned this lesson the hard way. Yes, it's time consuming when you have to shoe-horn one of these patients into an already booked schedule. But in the field of facial injectables, where a 3-dimensional appreciation is nearly always a factor in diagnosis, nothing replaces a face-to-face office visit. Photos and videos only provide two dimensions and the effect of lighting and camera angle cannot be overstated. To drive the point home, I'll state it again: patients and practitioners speak two different languages.

PRACTITIONER - PATIENT DIALOGUE

To ultimately arrive at the patient's precise area of concern and its treatment possibilities our responsibility as practitioners requires that we alternate between information-seeking and information-giving. Dialogue is pivotal. In truth, the esthetic outcome and patient satisfaction relies heavily on your ability to encourage discussion and communicate effectively. I'll say it again - no industry jargon.

One of the essential objectives of the consultation discussion is to uncover a patient's motivation for treatment. This is fairly easy to reveal with a simple open-ended statement such as: *"How long have you been considering treatment and is there something particular that motivated you to schedule this appointment today?"* The literature is very clear on this matter. Treatment motivation driven by the notion that it will rescue a relationship, please someone other than themselves or enhance job prospects is dangerous and unrealistic. Patients falling in this category are extremely poor cosmetic candidates. If you're confronted with such a patient, you must let them know you won't be treating them. Moreover, you have to deliver this unwelcome news in a diplomatic way. Showing empathy never hurts. You can begin your sentence with something like: "I know this isn't what you want..." or "I can understand that this might be frustrating..." Then continue in a sincere, compassionate tone and explain that in your experience, you've found that people who express a similar motivation for treatment are largely unhappy with their final results. You may decide to add that, as a practitioner, your primary reason for including facial injectables in your practice is to help people feel better and more positive about their appearance. Knowing this, you can't in good conscience go forward with treatment. Whichever way you decide to handle it, be sure your decision to not treat is conveyed without ambiguity. If there is any doubt in the patient's mind, they'll be back asking again and again.

Body dysmorphia is an absolute contraindication for cosmetic treatment. As mentioned, a full discussion of this topic goes outside the scope of this book. You can find a primer on Body Dysmorphic Disorder at the Anxiety and Depression Association of America website.[16] (see footnote)

It should be obvious, but it bears mention that no one NEEDS cosmetic treatment. Therefore, before your injectable practice gets started, you should make a personal promise to avoid excessively demanding patients. These people will make your job miserable.

---

[16] https://adaa.org/understanding-anxiety/related-illnesses/other-related-conditions/body-dysmorphic-disorder-bdd

Facial injectables have limitations and are certainly not capable of changing a patient's temperament. Also, learn to recognize individuals with unrealistic expectations. When a patient arrives holding a picture of a famous person and tells you they want "*that nose*" or "*those lips*" be smart enough to decline treatment.

Chapter 13

KNOW YOUR LIMITATIONS

"Knowing your limits is a strength not a weakness."
Kim Harrison

Every time I evaluate a patient for potential treatment, I take a moment to ask myself one question: "Knowing what I know about this procedure and my skills, would I be comfortable having *me* treat *me*?" That's my litmus test. If the procedure moves outside of my knowledge and skill base, I refer the patient. *Primum non nocere.* Knowing your limitations is essential for a number of reasons: 1. No patient should ever suffer as a consequence of your lack of knowledge or skill, 2. Building an injectable practice is a brick by brick project and can easily be knocked down by bad reviews or spreading of bad will 3. Litigation is something to be avoided 4. Your injectable practice should bring you joy, not frustration.

Most, if not all practitioners won't feel comfortable or confident after only one exposure to injectable training. It's nothing to be ashamed of. Don't be reluctant or embarrassed about taking multiple beginner level courses. It's the only way to become a confident and competent injector. With that said, the lowest risk procedure in the field of injectables is neurotoxins. It's helpful to start there and then move on with other modalities after you've had more instruction. Remember, be sure to treat staff and family whenever possible. Not only does it build your confidence but being able to see someone you've treated every day gives you real-time feedback and firsthand knowledge of how the treatment evolves. If facial injectables truly interests you, taking additional courses has to remain a priority.

Inevitably, once you've gained a patient's confidence, they'll try to talk you into performing other treatments that you're not comfortable with or that fall outside the limits of your license. Resist the urge to be a people-pleaser. If you're not trained, not confident or not permitted by the license you hold, don't let anyone coerce you into anything. Tempting though it may be, those risks are not worth taking. If something goes wrong and you get sued the Judge won't "pardon you" simply because the person begged you to do it. There's no dishonor in saying that something is not within your territory. I've declined many requests and I've never once regretted it. We have a responsibility as practitioners to practice within our orbit of education, competence and skill.

When Kybella first hit the market, I immediately got trained. It took two more training sessions along with independent study of the scientific literature before I treated my first patient. During that preparation period I had several patients ask me to treat them. My response was that I wanted more training before offering it in my practice. I even gave them referrals to core specialists who I knew were already doing Kybella in their offices. To my surprise, once I announced we were offering Kybella, these patients had been waiting in the wings and immediately queued up for treatment. They waited because they had total trust in me, knowing I wouldn't do anything without a complete understanding and solid training in the modality.

The lesson here is if you treat patients well and you stay within the boundaries of your competence you'll be rewarded by loyalty. It's the reality of life that mistakes will be made. But that likelihood increases whenever we encounter new or unusual circumstances. The difference between competence and incompetence is the variety and complexity of methods at your disposal to identify and treat problems as they arise. So, theoretically, the more exposure you have to these methods and situations, whether by independent study or traditional instruction, the more competent you'll become. Especially early in the evolution of any practice it's important to recognize and function within our limitations. Fortunately, limitations don't have to be permanent and can be overcome with commitment to training and education. Remember that trust takes time to build, seconds to break and forever to restore.

Like everything else, there are good courses and not-so-good courses. Beware of any and all training that portrays injectables as something that's so easy and risk-free that everyone should be doing it. That's patently false. In my opinion, this type of flashy promotion is used by overzealous purveyors of continuing education who are in the business of "selling" courses, or are themselves, unaware of the potential risks associated with some of these treatments. Caveat emptor!

Chapter 14

PHOTODOCUMENTATION

"Without proper self-evaluation, failure is inevitable."
John Wooden

Photodocumentation is an essential part of a successful facial injectable practice. It's rare that a non-core specialist would be very familiar and comfortable with facial photographic documentation. Yet, even for those with experience and training, taking quality photos for cosmetic documentation can be a challenge. It takes time, effort and commitment, but proper photodocumentation is a skill that you or your staff must do - and you must strive to do it well. The standard of care in facial cosmetic treatment includes pre- and post-treatment photographs. Beyond the fact that it's the standard of care, it's essential to know that once you pick up a syringe, there is no second chance to take a pre-treatment photograph. As your injectable practice grows, you'll come to know how critical these pictures can be. It's not unusual to find yourself obliged to prove you've made a visible difference in a patient's appearance. Research shows that we all have a more glowing perception of how we look than might be warranted.[17] Before and after photos are the only true way to demonstrate any treatment results.

---
[17] https://journals.sagepub.com/doi/abs/10.1177/0146167208318601?journalCode=pspc

I know this from having treatment myself. As a result of my erratic business travel schedule, finding time for my own facial injectable needs/wants can be a challenge. I usually wind up waiting longer than I should and then, just when I'm about to turn back into a pumpkin, I show up in my friend's office where he proceeds to inject no fewer than 5-6 ccs of dermal filler into my face. When the appointments over, I get in the car, look in the mirror and think, "*I don't look any different.*" OF COURSE I LOOK DIFFERENT! But our brain plays tricks on us. Likewise, our patients suffer the same perception-deception. The best way I know to make sure a patient can see these differences is to show them their before and after photos. Here's how we do this in my office: When the appointment is over, we ask the patients permission to email a before and after photo to them. But remember: DO NOT send photos to your patient without their consent. Additionally, you're duty-bound to send photographs encrypted since they fall under the heading of "patient records." Think about it, you don't want the patient opening an unexpected email at work with a coworker standing along-side them and staring right at their computer.

Unlike neurotoxins which take effect in ten to 14 days, dermal filler treatment results are seen immediately. With this being the case, I take post-treatment photos at the end of every dermal filler appointment. Usually in the evening after I'm done for the day, I look through the photos and select a before and after pose that best demonstrates what we've achieved for each patient. I stitch them together in a program such as Powerpoint to make them one file. If you leave them as separate files, the patient may have difficulty viewing them side by side on their computer or on their phone - which weakens your ability to showcase the effect. After my office sends the emails, nearly every patient winds up calling the office to thank us and say how pleased they are with their results. You can't underestimate the power of this easy step as a marketing tool and good clinical practice.

In addition to showcasing final results, there will be times when your pretreatment photo's save your hide. I've had this happen numerous times. Here's one example: One of my patients came in to have lower face rejuvenation with dermal fillers. This included her lips. As described, after we sent the photos to her, she called our office and was positively effusive about how much she loved her result. Bada-Bing! Right?? Not so fast. The next time she was in was some 5 or 6 months later. She reiterated how much she loved her result but added that since the treatment, she noticed she has *"some bluish marks on"* her *"lips that weren't there before."* I asked my nurse to pull up the patients' pretreatment photos on the computer, and lo and behold, there were the *"blue marks."* Of course, the patient replied that *she'd never noticed them before*. We're all guilty of not "seeing" some (maybe many) of our existing flaws. But do you think I'd ever be able to convince the patient that those "marks" were present prior to treatment without photographic proof? Not a chance! That's just one example when I've been "saved" by having quality pretreatment photographs. Never, ever omit this medico-legal step.

Another strong rationale for photo-documentation is practitioner self-improvement. When I first started offering injectables I rarely asked patients to return for the recommended 2-week follow-up evaluation after neuromodulator treatment. I felt sheepish and thought it was an imposition to ask busy patients to come back just so I can look at them. At some point I decided it was better to ask them to return than assume they'd call if their outcome was less than optimum. Moreover, the literature suggests that men are less inclined than women to return for commonly needed refinements such as eyebrow peaking (Mephisto sign) or inadequate Frontalis placement that leads to muscle recruitment at the Galeo-Frontalis juncture. It's important to identify and correct any of these common events both from a patient satisfaction and practitioner reputation point of view. Without a doubt, my skills enjoyed a dramatic quantum leap when I finally acted like an adult and instituted a 2-week follow-up after all first-time neurotoxin treatments. Only then could I see and evaluate my results. This singular small step led to a clear understanding of how to produce better outcomes for every case there-after. It was a real eye-opener that expanded my knowledge of how neurotoxins behave and without question, improved my overall injectable skills. Practitioner self-evaluation is a necessary step and easy to do when you have the ability to view before and after photographs side-by-side.

Chapter 15

THE DISSATISFIED PATIENT

"Your most unhappy customers are your greatest source of learning." Bill Gates

In Leo Tolstoy's book Anna Karenina, the first line reads *"All happy families are alike; each unhappy family is unhappy in its own way."* When you decide to add cosmetic treatments to your practice you have to be resigned to the occasional dissatisfied patient. I've found that in cosmetic treatment, "All happy patients are alike, but each unhappy patient is unhappy in his own way." I'll add to this premise that people who are generally unhappy in life are unlikely to be happy with their cosmetic results. However, there are times when patients have legitimate grievances. These findings will be visible to the practitioner as well. When this happens, we have an obligation to address the problem in a medically appropriate and prompt manner. Naturally, refinements should be done after the appropriate amount of time has passed to allow for resolution of bruising, swelling and for pharmacologic effect to be complete. Denying the problem exists or telling the patient it'll resolve on its own, when you know it won't, will only make matters worse. It creates chronic misery for you and your staff and has the potential to damage your reputation. Every patient is your advertisement - you don't want negative publicity for your office walking around or leaving bad feedback about you on the web.

Dealing with dissatisfied cosmetic patients is wholly unlike our non-cosmetic treatment patients. Cosmetic patient grievances can have a disproportionately weighty impact on you, your staff and your office atmosphere. Whenever possible, identify the patient who's a poor candidate for treatment based on what you can glean from their psychology alone and don't treat them. Bitter people make for bitter patients. Don't delude yourself into believing your exceptional charms can transform a wolf into a poodle. Find a way to refer that patient out of your office for treatment. Here are a few things you can say:

1. Jane, as you probably know, each procedure presents different challenges. In your case I don't think I'm the best person to do this procedure for you.
2. I don't think you and I share the same esthetic vision. Many people are capable of performing this procedure, and in your case, it's probably best done by someone who shares your vision.
3. David, I know you have your Botox done at other offices. In my practice, I prefer to treat patients who I treat consistently - this allows me to know when your last treatment was and how many units you received and where the units are placed. Since you don't mind being treated at multiple practices, I'm sorry to say we're not a good fit.

I came to a point in my career, and in life, when I decided that no one is permitted to waste my time. I resolved that if a patient I've treated presents a complaint to me, even if I disagree with their premise, I'll listen and fully embrace what they say. I've decided to find something, anything, that they say and learn from it. Even if I judge them to be unreasonable - I'll take away something useful so that the encounter is worth my time. This promise to myself has helped me grow as a practitioner and keeps me moving forward with a positive framework. I'll share an example with you.

Some years ago, (before learning the hard lessons and making the commitment not to treat people I didn't like or who I knew to be bellyachers) a bona fide nitpicking patient of my dental practice, inquired about dermal fillers. Knowing she had the ability to be a true fly-in-the-ointment I should have immediately shut her down and referred her out. But I didn't. Our conversation regarding her treatment centered around her concern that she didn't want to look "done." At that time, I was in the habit of quoting filler treatment fees by estimating the number of syringes I believed were needed to address the area. I told the patient that we could begin slowly and start with just one syringe which would create a very gradual change. I also made it plain to her that for full correction she'd ultimately need about 3 syringes. She agreed to begin with one syringe. At her follow-up visit I could see she was less than thrilled. (*surprise*!) She said she didn't see a difference. I showed her the before and after pictures, which admittedly didn't demonstrate a dramatic difference, but there was, for sure, a perceptible change. I reminded her of our pre-treatment conversation when I told her she'd need multiple syringes and that it was <u>her</u> decision to begin slowly. Trust me, this was a difficult discussion because she was clearly irritated. But here's the gold I was able to mine out of that exchange: She said, "If I can't see the difference after one syringe, what guarantee do I have that I'll see a difference after the next syringe?" I told her, "you're right, there's no way I can guarantee that." So, we agreed that we wouldn't go any further. She was still a major sourpuss and ultimately left the dental practice (*small favors*). But in the end, she didn't waste my time. She was absolutely right that I couldn't guarantee she'd see a difference. That conversation led me to change my approach to the office dermal filler fee structure. I no longer quote fees based on the patient knowing the number of syringes I planned to use. I decided that my fee is based on how much product I believe I'll need to bring the patient to a level of correction they desire and factor in my time and expertise. This completely revamps the common perception that dermal filler is just a commodity. I placed dermal filler back where I believe it belongs - as a medical procedure.

The lesson I took away from an unpleasant patient and a difficult encounter ultimately transformed my dermal filler practice. No more discussion of syringes, no patient concerns about left-over product, nothing. I feel appropriately compensated for my time and skill and the patient receives the appropriate treatment. Win-win.

Chapter 16

JOIN THE GROUP

"Do I not destroy my enemies when I make them my friends?"
Abraham Lincoln

There comes a time in every practice's evolution when sales calls feel like intrusions on an already overbooked schedule. As a matter of necessity and practicality, in a mature and bustling office, visits by product sales representatives usually wind up being relegated to support staff. The reality of any business is: time spent with a sales rep is time away from the patients who pay our bills. This means that the relationship a mature practice has with product salesmen is mainly through staff.

Even if you're in a fully developed practice, when you add injectables, that segment of the business is in an early stage of development. If you expect it to grow you have to be willing to commit the necessary resources - and sometimes that means <u>your</u> time. In the cosmetic industry there's a lot to be gained by cultivating a good relationship with injectable supplier reps - and it goes beyond the products they sell. First of all, these folks visit all the offices in your area (their territory) and have broad knowledge of your local market.

Their insight of the territory isn't based on hearsay - sales reps have the hard data. They know who's crushing it based on order histories. After forming a relationship with them you can pick their brains and ask if they'd recommend any successful growth strategies they may have seen at other offices. You can also ask them about the price range for services in your market. Treat them well and you'll find they're willing to help you. When you meet with them listen to what they say and be open to new information. These people are industry specialists who view what we do from a different angle - and that can be very helpful.

When I first started offering injectables my Allergan Rep invited me to an informational dinner hosted at a local restaurant. I was eager to attend, even though I wouldn't know anyone there. Back then I was one of only a handful of dentists doing injectables in my state. Not surprising, the attendees were predominantly core specialists - derms and plastics - and to say I was an oddity was putting it mildly. Before the lecture and dinner started there was a brief cocktail/mingle session. In the course of conversation if someone found out I was a dentist I could see the look of confusion flash over their face. Some people flat-out asked why I was there. Despite the initial feelings of being a misfit I continued to show up at nearly all local events held by Allergan, and at other company events as well. Soon, I got to know the regulars who attended and the "zoo-animal gawking" stopped. I began to feel more welcome and I'm really glad I persevered. Depending on the topic, these events can include live patient treatment demonstrations, new product rollouts, or new data presentations. No matter what's presented, these events are the only way I know of where a non-core specialist can meet and ultimately become part of the local cosmetic community.

Early on I could see that the specialists (dermatology, facial plastics and oculoplastics) were concerned I might be a threat to their territory. But as time went on, they realized that rather than "stealing their injectable patients" I became a new and robust source of referrals for them. Before starting my injectable practice, the only medical specialty I referred to with any consistency was dermatology - and that was maybe once or twice a year. Now, it's a weekly occurrence - and it's to all the core specialists.

Injectables can take a patient only so far - meaning it can't be the only approach used to address the elements of facial aging. Once you get to a certain point of correction you have to employ other modalities like surgery or laser. If only one treatment method is used, the patient begins to look bizarre. This is what I mean: as time progresses, you can't exclusively treat volume deficits and hyperkinetic muscles and ignore everything else that's going on. You have to address the other age-related problems as well. It's a lot like landscaping your home. You can have a nice-looking piece of property if you mow your lawn regularly, but to truly make an impact you'll need to have edging, trimmed shrubs, weeding, and tree pruning. Similarly, skin color, texture, tightness, as well as skin ptosis and redundancy are at present, largely out of reach by injectables. When one of my patients requires these services, since I don't do surgery or laser treatments, they have to be referred to someone else. Once you start an injectable practice, patients look to you for guidance on these matters. A trusted, reliable network of specialists becomes indispensable to any injectable practice.

Chapter 17

CREATING PATIENT AWARENESS

"Doing business without advertising is like winking at a girl in the dark. You know what you're doing but nobody else does."
Stuart H. Britt

When I first started offering injectables I had no grand plan of it growing into what it's become. In fact, looking back on it now, I didn't have much of a plan at all. What I did have was a natural curiosity and genuine interest in the human face, its beauty and facial aging. The extent of my ambition was to offer injectable services to a few women in the practice who had already voiced their interest. I was stunned when it began to grow organically. In short order, it became clear that this was a flourishing and financially rewarding component of my practice with untapped potential. That's when I took a greater interest in how I could nurture its growth even further.

Despite the obvious growth prospects, the reality is that I'm a small boutique practice with a very limited marketing budget. I started out small by asking my injectable supply representatives for professional advertising material for my office. Reps drive around with a ton of promotional materials in their cars that they're only too happy to get rid of. I looked at what they gave me and divided it up into what might be a "fit" for my office and what should get tossed. Next, I needed to consider the optimum location for the materials I kept. Believe it or not, the patient restroom turned out to be an excellent location due to its small area and limited wall space. Anything that goes on that wall, by default, gets attention. I was careful not to overplay the office advertising. In order to be strategic and judicious I sat in all the office seating that's designated for patients. Looking from those vantage points I was able to identify where eyes naturally landed. This included walls and surfaces such as counters and coffee tables.

When your sales rep gives you marketing materials, even if the entire inventory is attractive, don't feel compelled to overwhelm the office with promotional ads. Too much begins to look pushy and even desperate. Keep the materials you like and create a rotation with the display ads that you believe to be a good fit for your office.

Chapter 18

MARKETING TO YOUR EXISTING BASE

"Sell the problem you solve. Not the product." Unknown

An existing practice base is the easiest and most cost-effective place to begin your marketing focus. Patients currently in your practice are there because they already know, like and trust you. But before launching a marketing plan you have to consider who your patients are and what type of treatments they've been getting from you in the past. Why is this important? This isn't a book on marketing and I'm not a marketing expert, but as business owners we all need to know a few basics. The next paragraph explains one of the concepts you should understand before advertising.

It's probably obvious that, in order to sell a product or service, it needs to be relevant and hold some appeal to the target audience. For example, a marketing campaign centered around yard care equipment such as lawnmowers, leaf blowers and hedge trimmers, wouldn't be overwhelmingly successful if the advertising effort focused on an audience of apartment dwellers. This illustrates something called "Market Segmentation." Simply put, Market Segmentation evaluates consumers and divides them up according to demographics, common behaviors and interests. Recognizing who your current patients are, their interests, likes and dislikes allows you to understand them and thereby speak to them in a more natural way. Above all, it allows you to figure out if they might be interested in services that differ from those you currently offer. As consumers, we've all been on the receiving end of unwanted advertising whether on TV, radio, email or even snail mail. If you're like most people, you find these commercials to be annoying and intrusive. Savvy marketers know this and strive to use a more targeted approach. Sending irrelevant information (spam) to an unreceptive audience has the potential to make them angry. It goes without saying that pissing off your existing customers is very bad for business.

With this basic understanding of Market Segmentation, we can return to our discussion about advertising to your existing practice. How patients react to adding facial injectables in your office depends largely on whether the focus of your existing business can be viewed as complementary to cosmetic treatment. If your current practice centers on treatments associated with esthetics or beauty, the conversion is fairly easy. However, it might be confusing to the consumer if the type of healthcare you provide appears, in the patients' mind, unrelated. For instance, pediatric practices may have a more difficult challenge establishing a logical connection between their core practice of children's needs and traditionally adult-focused cosmetic treatments. There could be too many conflicting cues to allow the creation of a natural link. In cases like this, a patient might think the doctor is acting out of greed and is attempting to use injectables as a money maker. Another interpretation is that the practice is failing and desperate for a quick infusion of cash. But for most practices, if you can identify a potential need and desire within your patient base and injectables appear complementary to the services you already provide, internal marketing can be straightforward and cost effective.

Chapter 19

EMAIL MARKETING

"90% of Marketing doesn't work because it doesn't get done."
Neil Bradman

Moving beyond the physical advertisements inside your office, another way to let your patients know about your new treatment offerings is through your practice email base. Probably because most of us aren't marketers, the immense value of an email list is frequently overlooked by medical professionals. Think about it: unlike Social Media which is wide-open for all to see, email is private. This personal nature of email allows conversations to occur discreetly. It's not a public forum on a newsfeed and it's not subject to ever-changing algorithms that can affect the user experience. When you own an email list you run the show. It's the ultimate messaging freedom.

Market Segmentation of patients within your practice is extremely helpful when creating email campaigns. Studies prove that segmented emails are more effective than non-segmented.[18] As professionals, most of us check and are responsive to our email multiple times during the day. Unfortunately, not everyone is so

---

[18] https://myemma.com/strategy/eighteen-stats

inclined. Even though it seems like it would be a surefire way to inform your patients about your new services, email should be used as only a slice of your overall strategy - not the main ingredient. According to ConstantContact, open rates for emails coming from physicians and dentists average only around 14%[19]. - this ranks below the 20% average open rate for every other industry.[20] Email campaigns may well be inexpensive and require minimal effort but they're not the high-yielding proposition we'd love for them to be.

It's important to know that of the 14% that *do* open those emails, between 35-61% are viewing it on their mobile device. If you don't optimize your email for mobile, the majority of recipients (70%[21]) will immediately delete it! So, if you decide to go the email route, make it worth your while by having your content optimized for mobile. This should be an easy step if you're using any one of the patient relationship managing (PRM) software companies (SolutionReach, Weave, DocMate, etc). In fact, most of these companies offer the ability to create segmented groups within your database. For example, you might decide to create a group that is female, age 35-55 and lives within a certain zip code. It's really helpful when you know who your perfect customer is - your customer Persona. (more on Persona's later) You can create messaging that specifically targets and speaks directly to them. It's even possible to further divide those groups and send different email campaigns that would be more appropriately messaged for the selected demographic.

Understanding how well your email messages resonate with your audience is key. If you know something is working well, or not

---

[19] https://knowledgebase.constantcontact.com/articles/KnowledgeBase/5409-average-industry-rates?lang=en_US
[20] https://mailchimp.com/resources/email-marketing-benchmarks/
[21] https://www.superoffice.com/blog/email-open-rates/

working at all, that's incredibly valuable when creating your next campaign. Often, your PRM software will allow you to see click-through-rates (CTR). This is the percent of people that click on a link or ad in an email campaign. Your CTR is a super-helpful statistic that can be used to measure how well a particular campaign is performing. You can tweak your message or graphic and do A/B testing to see which rendition provides the highest CTR. The main factors that drive a reader to convert, *or click-through*, are relevance and opportunity. If the offer is relevant and well-timed that usually translates to conversion. This always reverts back to understanding your customer. If you know that client well, the ability to create content that resonates is so much easier.

Relevance of messaging is completely within our control. Injectable treatments are highly personal and a decision to pursue treatment involves logic and emotion. Good messaging should use imagery and words that attempt to satisfy these two states of mind. Timing is one of those parameters that serious marketers tend to obsess over. There's a lot of contradictory data when it comes to parsing out sweet spots for exact time of day to achieve maximum opening rate. Since optimum time of day can be a moving target, I tend to not focus on it as much as I do messaging. Timing can also relate to consumer receptivity. - which is usually beyond our control. So, our best bet is to attempt to appeal to the potential relevance of our message in a select segment of our practice.

Without a doubt, incentivizing your emails with an offer can increase your CTR. But here's my take on this. We've already discussed my view of discounts for new and existing patients in chapter 10. With the exceptions previously mentioned, I'm not a big fan of discounting cosmetic procedure fees for many reasons, but here's just one: Think of this from an optical point of view - Rather than discounting your fees (which can make your everyday fees appear artificially inflated) it might look better to offer something special for a limited time to a small number of responders. For example, *"For the first 10 respondents we're offering 2 oz of {insert brand name} facial cream complementary with any dermal filler treatment. Offer expires September 1st."* You can do this with any product, sunscreen, facial cleanser, etc. Avoid offering gift cards for unrelated items, like Starbucks or Amazon. Promotional items should be Brand-related to maintain a semblance of professionalism. As thrilling as it may be to host giveaways, resist the urge to be the Goodie-God or -Goddess. You don't want to overdo giveaways because urgency messaging is incongruous with medical services and can come off as desperate. With all that said, occasionally offering a small but relevant gift can stimulate patient interest without looking like the healthcare equivalent of a discount retailer.

If your office has a monthly newsletter, new treatment offerings are a perfect inclusion and a great way to create awareness. The same principles that apply to emails are applicable in newsletters as well. Here's a quick synopsis:

- Be sure the newsletter is formatted for mobile consumption (see footnote[22] for help with formatting)
- Keep newsletter topics thematic so they aren't confusing
- Balance the content: 90% educational/10% promotional
- Provide alternative text for any graphics you include to allow mobile users to understand what they're missing when blank spaces appear on their device
- Deliver personalized content for your Segmented Markets

---

[22] https://www.hostgator.com/blog/how-make-website-mobile-friendly/

- Test and optimize the content (headlines, design, layout, etc.), to determine what works best with each Segmented Market

Chapter 20

YOUR WEBSITE

"Never allow yourself to be defined by someone else's opinion of you." Unknown

Anyone expecting to grow a cosmetic practice, or any business for that matter, must have an online presence. A practice website is the one place on the net where you have complete control over the content describing you and your business. Today, our lives are firmly tethered to the digital world with nearly every man, woman and child carrying a cell phone. It defies all logic why any medical or dental practice would not have a website. If you've been in practice for more than six months, chances are you exist on the web. Data about you surfaces from government sites, state licensing boards, doctor rating sites, social network engines, real estate records, you name it. The question is: how accurate is that information? Are you willing to allow a patient you may have met once, define you? Wouldn't it be preferable to have control over how you and your practice are characterized?

This is why you need a website. You should take full advantage of this mechanism of advertising while being careful not to wade into the unseemly area of pompous or arrogant. Factual descriptions of your expertise are helpful and appreciated by prospective patients. Bragging, on the other hand, is interpreted as self-important and conceited. Intentionally exaggerating your experience in hopes of impressing the reader is not only unethical but comes off as snooty and insulting. Your website exists, in part, to amplify the "know, like and trust" factors that influence a prospective patient's decision to choose you. Don't underestimate the selling power of a well-designed website. A 2018 survey of over 1700 US adults showed that 63% of respondents reported choosing one practitioner over another because of a stronger online presence.[23]

Remember, first impressions matter. Unless you have experience, time, and you're really good at it, don't build your own website. Hire a professional. Think of your website like the lobby of a hotel. The minute you step inside you know which brand category you've entered. The furniture, the lighting, the staff - all provide visual cues as to whether you're inside the Motel 6 or the Four Seasons. Depending on what type of experience you're looking for, one look around and you know if you're in the right place or not - and whether you want to stay. If your website is outdated, takes too long to load, has multiple unrelated fonts and clunky navigation, say goodbye to your prospective cosmetic patient. Your messaging and content should present a professional, uncluttered image that invites and pleases the eye. The style and vibe of your site is a reflection of your esthetic discernment. Don't miss this chance to establish a great first impression.

In addition to an attractive, user-friendly landing page your website should include an "About Us" page. This is where you can present

---

[23] https://www.doctor.com/cxtrends2018

information such as how long you've been in healthcare, educational background, professional activities, practice philosophy and if you choose, some carefully curated personal data. Make sure your practice location and contact information is easy to find on every page. There's nothing more maddening than having to jump from tab to tab desperately searching for the office location or phone number. Another critical element is making sure to optimize your website for mobile use. Mobile web traffic surpassed desktop and laptop traffic in 2014 and continues trending in that direction.[24] Think of how many times you've attempted to access a site on your phone and aborted the mission due to lack of functionality. Each one of those abandoned searches represents a missed opportunity or sale for the website owner. Don't be that guy.

---

[24] https://www.broadbandsearch.net/blog/mobile-desktop-internet-usage-statistics

Chapter 21

ONLINE REVIEWS

"Brand is just a perception, and perception will match reality over time." Elon Musk

Beyond your website, online reviews are the top go-to destinations where prospective patients head to learn more about you. Like it or not, most people trust online reviews from strangers because they see the reviewers as peers.[25] Since these opinions are valued as much as personal recommendations, they can have a direct impact on your bottom line. One survey reported that up to 60% of people selected a doctor based on positive online reviews.[26] Although doctor-rating specific sites exist, Yelp is probably the most frequently thought of and familiar site. It's incumbent upon all of us to monitor our online reputations.

So, what happens if you get a bad Yelp? If you get a bad review - pause. Don't answer right away, you're likely to say something that sounds angry or unprofessional. Keep in mind that the rules of online engagement for medicine are completely different than those of any other form of commerce. Most sources recommend that you wait a bit, perhaps a full day and then call the patient or maybe send a note of apology if it seems appropriate.[27] It's not a good idea to reply

---

[25] https://www.marketwatch.com/story/this-is-exactly-how-many-reviews-it-takes-to-get-someone-to-buy-something-2017-08-22-12883123

[26] https://www.doctor.com/cxtrends2018

online to bad reviews without the advice of a trusted attorney. As much as it's gut-wrenching to stand idly by while a negative review is sitting out there for all the world to see, jumping in with a poorly worded response can make matters much worse. For now, we have to accept that the world of online reviews is not a level playing field in healthcare. We're beholden to the laws of HIPAA, and even if the patient identifies himself, as practitioners we cannot disclose any information about the patient without their permission. The potential liability stakes are so high that it's really ill-advised to do anything without good legal advice.

Unfortunately, no matter how kind and careful you are as a practitioner there's always the risk of a lousy review. How do we manage an online image when the rules of engagement are stacked against us? Is there a recommended strategy for wading through the tortuous waters of online reviews? It's been said that the best defense is a good offense. Without a doubt, if you have only one review, and it's a bad one, you're in a difficult spot. But if you have ten reviews and only one is bad, that's very different. Most readers are able to put one bad review out of ten good reviews into proper perspective. Furthermore, one negative testimonial in fifty often suggests more about a disgruntled reviewer than it does about the business being reviewed. With that in mind, it should seem obvious that you need to find a way to get positive reviews. Simple, right? But if you're like most practitioners, asking a patient for a review feels "icky" and finding a way to do it tactfully and professionally is baffling.

When you think about the psychology of a potential reviewer the prospect becomes less daunting. Reviewers are just like us. In fact, many of us have reviewed restaurants, hotels, or service-people and

---

[27] https://www.ama-assn.org/delivering-care/patient-support-advocacy/how-respond-bad-online-reviews

possibly even other practitioners. Unfortunately, motivation to leave a review is usually the consequence of an intense emotional response - either positive or negative. And, how many times have you promised yourself that you'd leave a review and then forgot about it? Let's face it, there are far too many distractions and more interesting things to do in life. That's why sites like TripAdvisor do their best to incentivize would-be reviewers. Appealing to our innate competitive nature, consumer review platforms like TripAdvisor "gamify" the reviewer experience by awarding badges, keeping track of "points" and displays the number of "helpful votes" a reviewer receives. Understanding that out-of-sight means out-of-mind, they send their contributors weekly email reminders with a call to action (CTA), asking for more reviews.

Identifying the friction points that prevent patients from posting reviews allows you to create a smooth passage around potential obstacles. The two most common barriers to leaving a review are 1. Remembering to leave a review and 2. Where to post the review. If you can remove those two impediments, you're more than half-way there. Once I realized this, the solution was easy. I created a handout. On simple 3 x 5 index cards I printed the "where" and the "why." (link for customizable template and instructions download: **bit.ly/PracticeForms**). To be honest, I originally created these for my injectable teaching business before it dawned on me, I could use them in my practice. Here's how it evolved: Even though my educational organization had been up and running successfully for a few years, we weren't getting reviews. Occasionally I'd remember to ask, but most people forgot about my request as soon as they left the building. I knew I needed to find a way to help them remember and make it so easy that it was almost unavoidable.

After designing index cards that included all the necessary information, I printed out a stack of them and took them to our events. My staff was fully aware and supportive of how we planned to use these. During the session they were charged with evaluating participants with the goal of identifying anyone who seemed exceptionally pleased with the course. Often these turned out to be people who had taken a course from another organization and therefore had a basis for comparison. As we neared the end of a training session, my staff and I would discuss who we thought would be our best ambassadors. Once we agreed, I personally would speak with that candidate and explain to them that we were trying to grow our Social Media presence and asked if they'd be willing to write a review for us. If they agreed and I still had a good vibe I'd walk over to my computer bag and grab one of the index cards and hand it to them.

It's impossible to overstate how important it is to screen prospective reviewers. You should develop your own set of criteria and be sure to get staff consensus on patients you select. If a staff member has a spidey-sense that the person might not be a good candidate, it's best to abandon that one and wait for a more suitable contender. Remember that patients often reveal personality traits in front of your staff that they manage to hide from you. When it comes to queasy sensations, go with your gut. It's rarely wrong. Consistently ask for reviews from patients who'll provide positive feedback and you'll establish a powerful antidote to the inevitable hater that pops up.

REVIEW PLATFORMS

It's the rare business that takes time to read the terms of use before signing up or participating in online review sites and forums. More often than not, users become aware of a platforms terms and conditions after they've committed a violation and have their account suspended. It's true that Yelp's official statement is that they discourage the practice of businesses asking for reviews. However, if you dig deeper they say that asking for reviews does not violate their terms of service, but it IS a violation if you incentivize a review with some form of compensation.[28] So, if you don't offer any type of reward, you're not in violation. Even if it's not Yelp, I strongly advise that you never provide an incentive for a review. Think of all the ways that financial incentives can be a problem for a review. First, a patient may feel obliged to give a more glowing review when they know they're being compensated. Second, if potential consumers learn that reviews are paid for, every positive review is thrown into question. Trust is lost - along with that potential patient.

---

[28] https://marketingland.com/5-yelp-facts-business-owners-should-know-163054

Chapter 22

SOCIAL MEDIA

"Social Media is one area of business where you don't need to outspend your competitors in order to beat them." Hal Stokes

What exactly do we mean by "Social Media?" It's really an evolving term, but to put it broadly, Social Media are internet-based tools that allow the user to interact with (or passively observe) individuals and groups. It allows us to share information, images, videos and any digital content, often in real time. There are hundreds of platforms but at the moment, the current major players are Facebook, Instagram, YouTube and Twitter - although Twitter is now self-identifying as a "news app" in the iOS App store rather than a social networking application. The dominant actors of today are certain to evolve and change with time.

According to Social Media Examiner[29] about 40% (3 Billion people) were active on Social Media channels in 2019. Moreover, according to BroadBandSearch, the average person is projected to spend more than a collective 2 hours on social networking each day in 2019.[30] To forego a presence in these social spaces, where much of your content

---
[29] https://www.socialmediaexaminer.com/
[30] https://www.broadbandsearch.net/blog/average-daily-time-on-social-media

can be placed and consumed for free, is definitely a missed opportunity to tell your story and establish your brand.[31] Furthermore, in all likelihood your competitors are active in these spaces and engaging with the same audience you'd like to recruit. Turning your back on Social Media because of apathy or indifference not only makes you appear to be a luddite, it's a missed opportunity when you're trying to build or expand a business.

Once you elect to participate in Social Media you have to decide on a clear objective. Business goals for Social Media utilization can and do vary. Since medical practitioners rarely sell products online, a typical marketing goal is to create Brand awareness and inspire Brand loyalty. Another could be to educate and engage your audience. Often, practices simply want to turn their Social Media audience into advocates of their Brand. Whatever your reason, without establishing a defined goal for Social Media marketing, your posts become disjointed and your messaging is often confusing.

Before you download an app and create a profile on any platform, be sure to write down your goals and how you plan to achieve them. This serves as a guiding purpose and provides clear direction for you or whomever is in charge of creating your content. If you can't easily articulate this mission to (yourself or) whomever is tasked with the content creation, you need to spend more time reflecting on your "why." For example, let's suppose one of your goals is to create Brand awareness and drive potential patients to your website. A way to measure that would be to use Google Analytics[32] which shows your website traffic and where it's coming from. To use this tool most effectively, plan on evaluating not just the overall traffic percentage received but when it's happening. Studying your traffic spikes or dips

---

[31] https://www.lyfemarketing.com/blog/marketing-through-social-media/
[32] https://marketingplatform.google.com/about/analytics/

and their association with content will help you create and modify messaging that's effective and achieves your aims. Understand this: without a clear "why" your content will lack purpose and fail to provide value to your audience. Posts that aren't intentional are the equivalent of throwing something against a wall and waiting to see what sticks. That's a waste of time - and in the end, time is always money.

Once you've decided on the "why" (your goal) of your Social Media presence, the next task is to determine the "who." This is the audience you want to engage. Zeroing-in on who you're trying to reach makes content creation much easier and in turn, moves you closer to your goals. So how do you find your audience?

Imagine that a Social Media Channel (Instagram, Facebook, etc.) is a telephone. To advertise you'd like to use that phone to speak with your audience. In your quest to make it worthwhile and reach a large group, you might decide to dial-in to a massive conference call. But in fact, this could be a waste of time. Here's why: A random group of people whom you know nothing about, may or may not be looking for your services. In other words, an arbitrary group phone call is not strategic. By phoning in, you're hoping there are a few people who perchance, might be receptive to what you're saying. However, depending on who they are, their sex, demographics, age, etc., - what you say on that conference call might sound strange, irrelevant or even offensive to them. In the world of Social Media this would be like friending anyone and everyone, regardless of who they are, ignoring their potential interests (or lack-there-of), simply to have an audience to speak to. Obviously, this is weird, ineffective and could even be counterproductive. Rather than waste your time talking to people who don't care about what you have to say, wouldn't it be better to know the phone numbers of people who would be receptive or potentially interested in your message? That is your target customer (patient)! In marketing terms this is called Persona Development. The value of creating your Patient Persona is that it helps you construct intentional and effective content that speaks directly to THEM in terms they understand. Once you have a good idea of who your end user is, it becomes much easier to tailor your posts exactly to their needs and wants.

Here are a few things to consider when you're creating your Patient Persona:

Take some time to think critically about your ideal customer. Who is this person? What is their average age, background, educational level, gender, spending habits, goals, needs, motivations and pain points? Create a list of all their characteristics. Once you've nailed down who this person is, search the internet for an image that you think closely represents your Persona and save it with their demographics. It's also helpful to give the Persona a name to use when discussing them with your Social Media team or staff (or just thinking about it on your own). Personas keep you focused on the desires of your target audience and help you develop a conversation with them. (head over to this link for a downloadable Persona Worksheet **bit.ly/PracticeForms**) As you begin to understand your Persona's behavior and he or she becomes more real to you and your staff, creating relevant and engaging content becomes easier. Think of it this way, advertising that appeals to a 28-year-old female working in upscale retail (perhaps Neiman Marcus) doesn't necessarily appeal to a 50-year-old female executive working at a fortune 500 company. Their ages and income make them very different markets and their esthetic needs are completely different.

Ultimately, clarifying "*who*" reveals the demographics of the group you want to engage. This, in turn, leads you to uncover where they hang out - meaning, in which social channels are they active? (Facebook, Instagram, Snapchat, YouTube, etc.) Since platforms are constantly popping up and existing ones change or fade away, you'll need to monitor the different sites and their demographics. SproutSocial[33] is a great place to find this information and can help steer you to the most appropriate platforms for you Social Media campaigns.

So, what should you post about? Think of it this way: What might you say at a cocktail party if you found yourself speaking to someone who might be in the market for injectables? Remember this, you become very boring when you talk only about yourself. People might be polite for a little while, but they won't hang around long once they figure out that you only talk about *you*. The same holds true with Social Media - people don't really care about you or how lovely your practice decor is or how many staff members you have. They care about what services you might offer that could benefit *them*. Look at your practice from a prospective-patient point of view. What questions or concerns does your target market have? Offering answers or insight to those concerns will naturally engage those individuals. Show them how you can solve their problem. Tailor your content to demonstrate that your practice exists expressly to manage issues similar to theirs every day. Your posts should inspire trust and credibility. But know this: Social Media marketing is a long game. Don't let one or two posts with zero likes or no engagement stop you from creating more content. By and large Social Media is free advertisement and can prove to be financially rewarding once you figure out how to use it to your advantage!

---

[33] https://sproutsocial.com/insights/new-social-media-demographics/

Depending on resources and whether you have resident talent in your office, you may be wearing all the Social Media management hats. In addition to setting the goals and defining the mission, you might also be the elected official in charge of content and posting. There's no shame in this. I personally do the lion's share of the Social Media management for my medical education company. But remember, everything can change on a dime and at some point, you might be handing over this assignment to someone else. It will save you time, frustration and help maintain consistent messaging if your plan is organized, targeted and in writing from its inception.

Before I understood the necessary framework of "why's, who's and personas" that I just shared with you, I personally had an exasperating "learning" experience when I attempted to hand over the content generation for my teaching organization to a graphic artist. Before getting started we talked briefly about who I felt my "target market" was, and I asked him to review what I'd already posted to get an idea of the content style I was looking for. That was it - *now go create!* To my utter frustration, I continuously found myself revamping the content he created. Sadly, the fault was all mine because I hadn't explained my strategy (goal) nor had I clearly defined who my target audience (Persona) was. If I'd only taken the time to establish all of this in writing (demographics, personal needs, desires, pain points, etc.) at the very beginning, it would have been as easy as handing a driver a road map. This small bit of planning could have saved hours of time, aggravation and money!

Should you opt to farm-out this responsibility, in addition to outlining a clear vision of who your target audience is, along with your goals, be absolutely certain that a consistent draft review protocol is in place. All drafts should be evaluated for HIPAA compliance. (more on

HIPAA later) And, no matter how good your instructions are nor how skilled this person may be, mistakes can be made. Grammar, misspellings and any other obvious bloopers represent subliminal cues to your audience about *you*. The smallest of flaws broadcast that you lack attention to detail. That's an unforgivable trait for someone who provides cosmetic treatments.

Chapter 23

SOCIAL MEDIA CONTENT CREATION

"Everything you post on Social Media impacts your Personal Brand. How do you want to be known?" Lisa Horn

"Content creation" is marketing language that simply means providing information to your target audience. That content is how we connect and build loyalty with those individuals. We rarely think about it, but there are subtle (and some not-so-subtle) differences in how we communicate with different people. For instance, you probably don't speak the same way to your 15-year-old son as you might to your 82-year-old mother. That's an extreme example but it illustrates the nuances associated with speaking to specific demographics on any given platform. Consider who your audience is when creating content and speak to them as you would if you were in the same room together, face-to-face.

First and foremost, when "talking" with your audience, be authentic. Remember how you were taught to write in school? Well, forget all of it. That style of writing is stilted and boring and NO ONE enjoys reading it. Moreover, it's completely devoid of individuality. Being authentic means communicating in a natural way without rigid and overly formal delivery. People respond positively to genuineness. Authentic people are usually looked at as confident, honest, kind and trustworthy. So be yourself - but be your BEST self. You're still expected to be professional. Don't post something you'll live to regret. If you have any doubt about a piece of content, before you post, run it by someone you trust to tell you the truth - even if you don't want to hear it.

In any business, including medicine, the reality is that you can't be all things to all people. Don't torture yourself over that lost potential patient and fixate on why they didn't pursue treatment with you. Yes, some self-reflection and honesty about your own behavior as a practitioner is always good. But obsessing over the one that got away is not going to help you in whatever task it is you need to focus on now. Direct your attention on who you *are* treating, not who you *could have* treated. In the words of Seth Godin: "Everyone is not your customer." Don't set out to be a pandemic people pleaser. Absolutely key to a successful injectable practice is also identifying who *isn't* your ideal patient. Staying focused on your ideal customer and speaking directly to them in your posts can help weed-out those less than ideal patients that you wouldn't benefit from having in your practice anyway.

Before you start creating content, think about how you personally use Social Media and what grabs your attention. In the course of human history no one has ever said, *"I love it when people try to sell me something!"* Keep that in mind when generating ideas for your posts. It's really important not to be too salesy with your content. People want to be entertained or educated when they're browsing. Self-promotion is repetitive and becomes very tedious very fast. People will either un-follow you or just tune you out. Create a rule for yourself that only 10-20% of your content (or about 1 in every 5 posts) is sales focused. Your other content should inspire, enlighten or entertain.

A few examples of content that might be interesting to your audience:

1. How long does Botox work?
2. New product information
3. What's the difference between Botox and dermal fillers?
4. What's the Botox Blowout?
5. What are the side effects of Kybella?

There's plenty of research and industry news that never finds its way to the public. Social Media is a good way for us to educate the public and create awareness. The ability to breakdown industry language into layman's terms is always welcome since it serves the need in each of us to be informed. When you post useful and enlightening information your followers leave your Social Media platform better educated and able to speak intelligently with their friends about the topic. Be sure your information is truthful. Don't try to make something sound better, easier or faster than it truly is - solely to close the next sale or book the next procedure. Recognize that, as practitioners, we're held to a higher standard. Never post hyped up news that's deceptive or misleading.[34]

Some Social Media channels are suitable sites for posting endorsements. Patient testimonials can be popular and engaging content as well as effective Brand reputation building. Of course, the patient should be comfortable with the intended post and agree - in writing - to allow you to use their statement. Research tells us that personal endorsements are powerful influencers of patient behavior.[35]

---

[34] American Medical Association. Opinion 9.6.1 Advertising and publicity. Code of Medical Ethics. https://www.ama-assn.org/delivering-care/advertising-publicity. Accessed February 23, 2018

[35] Nassab R, Navsaria H, Myers S, Frame J. Online marketing strategies of plastic surgeons and clinics: a comparative study of the United Kingdom and the United

But like anything lacking in variation, posting an unending stream of testimonials becomes boring and annoying to your regular followers and could motivate them to 'unfollow' you. For a more in-depth look at common guidelines surrounding patient testimonials please follow this link to the American Medical Association: *The AMA Code of Medical Ethics stipulates that testimonials of patients as to a physician's skill or the quality of his or her professional services should "reflect the results that patients with conditions comparable to the testimoniant's condition generally receive."*[36]

To sum it up, Social Media is a place where people congregate and talk. When you have a business, someone somewhere out there is talking about you. Don't allow your Brand Identity to be created by anyone other than you. You don't need to post multiple times daily but getting your own information out there and establishing your Brand is essential.

States. *Aesthet Surg J.* 2011;31(5):566-571.
[36] American Medical Association. Opinion 9.6.1 Advertising and publicity. *Code of Medical Ethics.* https://www.ama-assn.org/delivering-care/advertising-publicity. Accessed February 23, 2018

Chapter 24

STAFF AND SOCIAL NETWORKING

"Privacy is dead, and Social Media holds the smoking gun."
Pete Cashmore

I know this may seem goofy to the generation who, as babies, were handed smart phones instead of rattles to keep them happy and content, but personal and professional Social Media accounts should always be kept separate. This is important because *private* Social Media accounts can still be accessed by users who may not be "followers" or "friends." Unfortunately, not everyone understands this and other potentially damaging aspects of an online presence. Given this is the reality, it's helpful to hold an office meeting for a full discussion - before a mistake is made. Having a written policy outlining the office's position on staff and their personal social networking is highly recommended. Many of these rules might seem obvious to *you* but they may not be evident to your employees. Make it clear that: staff should not connect with patients via Social Media; they should never provide medical advice online; if a patient asks for professional guidance they should be advised to seek care from an appropriate physician or clinic; and staff should steer clear of patients who are posting about treatment they've had or their medical conditions.

You may be familiar with the "18 HIPAA Personal Identifiers." All health information is considered *protected health information* (PHI) when it includes a personal identifier. Here's the list of all 18:

- Names
- Dates, except year
- Telephone numbers
- Geographic data
- FAX numbers
- Social Security numbers
- Email addresses
- Medical record numbers
- Account numbers
- Health plan beneficiary numbers
- Certificate/license numbers
- Vehicle identifiers and serial numbers including license plates
- Web URLs
- Device identifiers and serial numbers
- Internet protocol addresses
- Full face photos and comparable images
- Biometric identifiers (i.e. retinal scan, fingerprints)
- Any unique identifying number or code

At your office meeting, distribute and review this list to make sure everyone's aware of these identifiers. Have a frank discussion about what is and isn't acceptable Social Media content and messaging. Explain that no one should be fooled by a keyboard's "delete" button. Nothing is ever permanently removed from the internet and can be recovered by computer geeks, especially in a legal proceeding. So, if you wouldn't discuss it in a crowded elevator, then don't put it out in the ether for the world to see. Any post, that so much as hints at divulging anything - however minor - about a patient, is clearly off limits.

And finally, so that there is no ambiguity, describe the potential penalties for any Social Media HIPAA violations. These can range from immediate termination, to loss of license and/or hefty fines. If having this conversation makes you queasy or you find it too distasteful to talk about with your staff, you should know that when healthcare professionals violate HIPAA, it's usually *the employer* that receives the penalty.[37] Hopefully that inspires you to be completely forthcoming when spelling out possible disciplinary actions and repercussions.

---

[37] https://www.hipaajournal.com/what-are-the-penalties-for-hipaa-violations-7096/

Chapter 25

SOCIAL MEDIA PLATFORM RULES

"Dear Internet Users: One day you will regret not reading me. Sincerely, Terms and Conditions." ...Unknown

Most users of Social Media are unaware that all social channels have Terms of Use we're obliged to agree to when signing up. Among other things, these terms describe the sites interpretation of inappropriate content such as nudity and graphic violence. Violation of any of these terms can lead to termination of service and even legal action. It's important to familiarize yourself with these terms before utilizing the platform. Another often overlooked rule is the *granting of rights clause*. Most Social Media outlets have policies granting themselves legal rights to ownership - effectively transferring ownership of your posts to them - this includes your photographs. When a patient gives you permission to post their photo they must understand that their rights can no longer be protected since the photo becomes the property of the Social Media Company.[38]

---

[38] Instagram. Terms of use. Available at: https://help.instagram.com. Accessed August 8 2019.

Twitter. Twitter privacy policy. Available at: https://twitter.com/privacy?lang=en. Accessed August 8, 2019.

Facebook. Terms of service. Available at: https://www.facebook.com/terms.php. Accessed August 8, 2019.

Snap, Inc. Terms of service. Available at: https://www.snap.com/en-US/terms/. Accessed August 8, 2019.

Essentially, they need to know that once that photo is posted, it's irrevocable.

The Federation of State Medical Boards as well as the American Medical Association and the General Medical Council of Great Britain are all in agreement with respect to the ethics surrounding patient privacy, informed consent and Social Media. For more information you should access the appropriate professional Board website where your license has been issued.

Managing several Social Media platforms is a daunting task. Using a "Dashboard" software such as Hootsuite to cross-post on multiple accounts is possible, but remember, each platform has its own vision or purpose along with a set of users who usually share some demographics unique to that site. Therefore, infusing the same content onto all your social accounts might not be appropriate. Consider how professional advertisers strategize television marketing efforts. When watching your favorite news channel, the commercials run on that network are often very different from, say, those you'd see on ESPN. That's because the wise marketer creates advertising that speaks specifically to the demographic expected to be watching that channel at that time of the day. It's no different with Social Media channels. In addition to missing the demographic mark and not resonating with the audience, cross-posting from channel to channel looks lazy to anyone who might follow you on both platforms. In fact, people who follow you on both platforms may opt to "unfollow" you on one or both channels since duplicate content can be annoying. Meredith Hill, CEO of The Gifted Traveler has said, "If you speak to everyone, you wind up speaking to no one."

Here's a quick and dirty way to distill how you might gear your content:

- **Facebook:** Videos, Upcoming Events
- **Instagram:** Stories, High-resolution photos, quotes
- **Twitter:** News, links to articles, GIFs
- **LinkedIn:** Company News, article links, jobs, professional content
- **Pinterest:** Photos, Infographics, guides

For a reliable and concise in-depth look at each social outlet go to SproutSocial at: https://sproutsocial.com/insights/new-social-media-demographics/)

Chapter 26

PATIENT PRIVACY

"If you think compliance is expensive, try non-compliance."
Former US Deputy Attorney General Paul McNulty

In the quest for relevant content creation it might seem logical to post before and after photos of patients that you've treated. After all, isn't that a great way to demonstrate potential outcomes as well as showcasing your injectable prowess? Well, yes and no. This is indeed an awesome way to educate patients but there are potentially serious legal privacy concerns and ramifications. Even if you believe the photo shows only a limited area and therefore "doesn't display the entire face for identification," you cannot legally display the picture without written consent from the patient.

HIPAA (Health Insurance Portability and Protection Act) or the Kennedy-Kassebaum Act was enacted in 1996 and was created largely to modernize the flow of healthcare information and to protect patients' rights and their personally identifiable information. Back in 1996 Snapchat, Facebook and Instagram didn't exist so there aren't any rules in the bill specific to Social Media. The laws and standards, however, apply directly to how we may or may not use patient photographs in our digital presence.

The days of placing a black rectangle over the eyes to conceal someone's identity are over. Anyone can make a very good case that they can be positively identified by either their nose, chin, lips or smile alone. Neither HIPAA nor any Privacy Rulings provide specific wording that relates to de-identifying patient photos. In the "Final Privacy Rule" of 2000 the US Department of Health and Human Services (DHHS) states that "...the only absolute requirement is the removal of full-face photographs."[39] At the time of this writing there are no standard guidelines on how to de-identify facial photos. In the absence of specific rules, to avoid the possibility of litigation it's essential to get written informed consent from the patient to lawfully use any of their photographs. And remember, patients must be informed that those rights are irrevocable.

In my private practice, every time a patient consents to injectable treatment they also sign a photographic consent. This form has layers of release. By that I mean the patient can selectively allow or deny me the ability to use their image in different ways. The most basic, and the one they all must agree to, allows me to keep their photos within their secure medical records. The other potential uses are:

- Electronically emailed to my treating health professional
- Reproduced for use in education and training presentations for healthcare professionals
- Used in paper or electronic health/medical publications
- Used in marketing materials
- Shared in Social Media or other digital media

---

[39] https://www.hhs.gov/sites/default/files/ocr/privacy/hipaa/administrative/privacyrule/prdecember2000all8parts.pdf?language=es

Even if they've signed off on each of these to allow full usage, should I decide to use their photos I have a direct one-on-one conversation with them. I fully discuss the nature of irrevocable release and I show them the exact photos I plan to use. Once they understand the intended use, I have them sign a fresh copy of the release where I've detailed in writing, which photos I'll use and for what purpose.

Chapter 27

5 IMMUTABLE RULES

In addition to everything we've covered in this book, there are five things I consider to be hard and fast rules when starting and running an injectable practice.

RULE #1: When you get trained, start injecting. Period.

In my years of teaching facial injectables I've noticed that certain practitioners attend a basic level training course and then two years later they're back at another beginner level course. I can definitely understand that in 2 years enough has changed in this young and evolving field, but these practitioners were there because they hadn't picked up a syringe in all that time. I wish I could identify these people in advance and speak with them before they ever enroll. Believe it or not there's actually a word for this. Socrates and Aristotle called it "Akrasia." A loose translation would be "procrastination." Essentially, it's whatever it is that keeps you from following through with your original intentions. Like many problems, if you can identify it - you can fix it.

If you want to make a sincere "go" at an injectable practice you've got to begin as soon as you're trained. You don't have to start with the complex cases - but you MUST start. Years ago when I opened the doors to my brand new dental practice, the man who owned my building said this to me: "It's going to be hard, but you have to start somewhere." I've never forgotten those words - nothing flowery, just the honest reality. If you don't start right after your training the chances of getting it going appear to decrease exponentially over time. You forget what you learned and one day you wake up and believe you've forgotten enough to where you're now incapable. Then, there you are - back to square one.

RULE #2: Anticipate Adverse Events/Side Effects

In the words of Rebecca Fitzgerald, MD - *"If you're not having adverse events, you're just not doing these procedures enough. We all have adverse events."* Shortly after I began injecting, I had a patient who developed brow ptosis after treating her with Botox. Of course, the wonderful thing about neurotoxins is that they ultimately wear off. Yes, her brow ptosis resolved but it could have been very easy to lose my confidence and say, "forget it. I'm done." When the goal is to make someone look better and they wind up looking temporarily worse, that's powerfully discouraging. But like everything else, the more we do something the better we become at it. All practices and specialties of medicine, dentistry and nursing involve the occasional adverse event or side effect. The human body is complex and replete with unique variations. If that were not the case, one size would fit all when prescribing any medication and all surgeries could be performed by robots without any human oversight. A less than perfect outcome isn't always the result of gross negligence. It's often the result of unforeseen human variations that are unknowable even with today's medical technology. Despite the imperfect information available in medicine, we all continue to do our absolute best. One minor adverse event should not end an entire career. If that were the case, there wouldn't be a practitioner left standing among us. Don't let minor side effects and adverse events derail you. Learn from your outcomes, think carefully about every case, and continue to advance your education. Make sure you understand how and why adverse events can occur and be prepared for them.

RULE #3: Discuss HIPAA compliance with staff - before you have a violation.

As discussed in chapter 26, it's up to the practitioner to make plain, the laws surrounding patient privacy and confidentiality. Assuming most adult employees fully understand either of these concepts is foolish and can be disastrous. If you haven't already had the discussion with your staff, now is the time. Hold an office meeting and explain the Federal HIPAA Laws and how they affect patient privacy. It's said that the road to hell is paved with good intentions. Posting before and after pictures on Social Media without a patient's informed consent and written permission is a blatant HIPAA violation. Well-meaning staff might not be aware of this - they see hundreds of examples of patient treatment photos posted by other offices on their social feed every day. Give your team concrete examples of what is not allowed. Be sure to discuss confidentiality policies and procedures as well as consequences of violation of these policies. I've heard many offices have a "zero-tolerance" policy resulting in immediate dismissal after any infraction. When I started my injectable practice, I had every employee sign a confidentiality agreement. I'm not an attorney - I can't tell you if these agreements offer indemnity to the practitioner or his/her office, however, having staff sign a document drives home the seriousness of these laws and consequences as well as providing you with an outline for the necessary discussion. {sample copy of policy can be found at: **bit.ly/PracticeForms**}

RULE #4: Don't limit injectable treatments to one day a week

As a way to economize on resources some practices institute "injectable only" days. While this type of scheduling is commonplace for procedures such as surgery, it doesn't work for injectables. Here's why: cosmetic *surgery* is a planned event. People don't wake up in the morning and call around to multiple offices asking if there are any openings that day for a facelift. Surgery requires planning, preparation, as well as special rooms, equipment and personnel. Surgeons usually have a formal arrangement with a hospital or center whereby a certain day of the week is dedicated to procedures that require a surgical suite and its specialized staff. Injectables are completely different. They don't require special facilities or staffing. Further, most patients don't need pre-treatment lab tests for injectables. More often than not, Botox is an "impulse" purchase. It works like this: someone's been thinking about having an injectable treatment for a while and then for whatever reason, that day they make the call. If your office has "injectable only" days that person may have to wait upwards of a full week before you can see them. When a patient calls it's an opportunity to strike while the iron is hot. If your office has a 2 or 3 day wait before they can be seen, and at my office we can see them today - who do you think they'll schedule with? And if I achieve their goals, they become my patient.

Think of it from the patient's perspective: if you only allow injectable appointments one day a week - that means your store is only open *one day a week*. Not only is that a major inconvenience for patients, it makes no business sense at all. In that model, you're paying for 7 days of office space and using it only one day out of seven. A smart person once said to me: "it will never be a full-time practice until you're there full-time." You should consider your injectable practice as a full-time endeavor and make every attempt to see injectable patients any day you're in the office. Patients demand flexibility in scheduling. Think about all the urgent matters that you squeeze into your schedule every day. Many of these emergency patients require attention that takes up 10-15 maybe 45 minutes of *your* time. Neuromodulators don't take 45 minutes of staff and/or practitioner time. Keep the doors open.

RULE #5: Store indispensable injectable information in a secure location that cannot be deleted or removed from the office

I applaud practitioners who bring their staff to continuing education courses and I believe it's absolutely key to practice growth success. But keep in mind the purpose of staff attendance is to play a much needed and valuable **support** role. Staff attendance at training events doesn't absolve the practitioner from fully understanding product preparation and handling. The doctor who doesn't commit to a complete understanding of this aspect because *"my staff will be taking care of that"* will find him/herself unable to treat injectable patients should that staff member be out sick or even quit altogether. Never allow your injectable practice to be put on hold (or end!) because a staff member left with the keys to the kingdom. Be absolutely sure that critical information needed for any aspect of your injectable practice is either in writing in a secure location or etched in your brain and used regularly. In my early practice years, I employed a receptionist who shared with me a list of curated contacts of local reliable service people (plumber, electrician, snow removal, etc.). All the names and numbers were entered into the office rolodex (my property) and kept at the front desk (also my property). She and I had a less than amicable departure and the next time I needed the list, you guessed it, Vanished!

Chapter 28

LET'S GO!

"The only skill that will be important in the 21st century is the skill of learning new skills. Everything else will become obsolete over time." Peter Drucker

Injectables are a transcendent departure from mainstream procedures performed daily by dentists and most medical specialists. For many of us, patients are usually seen in the office out of necessity and reluctant obligation. In truth, they'd much rather be anywhere else. But with cosmetic injectables, that negative bias evaporates. Suddenly we find ourselves treating patients who are happy to be in the chair - they actually *want* what we're offering! It's a completely different ethos, and a welcome one at that!

For the Type-A's in the crowd, myself included, nothing ever seems to happen fast enough. When you're in the thick of it, building a practice can feel like it's happening at a glacial pace. But, until you commit to the first step, your dream of having a thriving injectable practice is just that: a *dream*. If you're truly interested in adding facial injectables to your practice, get going. Now. Start by getting trained and making incremental changes to establish the injectable practice framework I've outlined in this book. Get your staff on board and their excitement will inspire and motivate you to stay on track. Remember, as you're starting out, be frugal with the things that don't make you a better injector. Be tenacious and never stop learning.

And finally, enjoy! - Take pleasure and personal satisfaction in the unique ability to help your patients look and feel like the best version of themselves.

As you reach the end of this book, I sincerely wish you the best in your journey as you set out to establish your injectable practice. If you feel this book has helped you on your way, I'd be thrilled to hear about your experience! Contact me at: comments@estheticseminar.com

Cheers!

Gigi

AFTERWORD

Over the past decade of teaching facial injectables, one of the most common questions I've been asked is how to get an injectable practice up and running. My courses are already densely packed with anatomy, pharmacology and skill training, (*all vital ingredients for a safe and competent injector*) therefore, **time** is a major limiting factor to any meaningful discussion on the business aspects of injectable practice development.

Results of our post-course surveys indicate a number of things. Without question, RULE #1 from chapter 27, stating that after training, you've got to start immediately, is a huge factor in launching a successful injectable practice. But equally impactful are the many other seemingly small, but significant barriers to entry, covered in this book. I've built a cosmetic injectable practice and I know how to navigate around all these obstacles - big and small. Here, in this guide, I can share my experience and provide complete answers to the business questions surrounding injectable practice creation and development.

Finally, I'd like to thank you, the reader, for joining me on this journey. I truly hope it's been helpful. If you have comments or suggestions for future editions of this book please feel free to email me at: comments@estheticsminars.com.

And, if you have a moment to spare, I'd greatly appreciate a review of this book on Amazon! (you already knew I'd ask!!)

Made in the USA
Monee, IL
09 July 2023

38831698R00080